UN-HIJACK YOURSELF:

How to Keep Your Cool in the Heat of Emotion

Lina Juodelyte

Un-Hijack Yourself: How to Keep Your Cool in
the Heat of Emotion in 4 Steps with R.I.D.E.
Juodelyte, Lina

Copyright © Lina Juodelyte 2021

All rights reserved. Without limiting the rights under copyright reserved above, no part of this publication may be reproduced, stored in or introduced into a database and retrieval system or transmitted in any form or any means (electronic, mechanical, photocopying, recording or otherwise) without the prior written permission of both the owner of copyright and the above publishers.

lina@emotionready.com

http://emotionready.com

Janis and Margaret - without you, this book wouldn't have made it to light. Thank you for your kind words even more than for your great edits.

Mama, Tėti ir Rūta - be jūsų, ši knyga nebūtų įmanoma, nes nebūčiau įmanoma aš. Ačiū už jūsų niekad nesusvyruojančią meilę.

Kat - thank you for the light you so generously share. It makes the world a better place.

TABLE OF CONTENTS

Introduction 1
How Do We Get Emotionally Overwhelmed? 14
    Amygdala Hijacking 16
    Emotional Overwhelm vs. Amygdala Hijacking 17
    Emotional Overwhelm Characteristics 19
        Summary 20
R.I.D.E. - Four Steps Out of Emotional Overwhelm 21
    Summary 29
Be Aware of These Three Traps 30
    Trap #1. Being a Victim 30
    Trap #2. I am right, and he is wrong 31
    Trap #3. I shouldn't be feeling this way. 32
        Summary 33
Step 1: R. - Recognize the signs early 35
    Triangle Tool to Master R. - Recognizing Signs 36
        Body 38
        Thoughts 39
        Emotions 41
    Six Case Studies of Emotional Overwhelm 43
        Overwhelming Anger 43
        Overwhelming Fear 45
        Overwhelming Embarrassment
        (Close to Shame and Even Disgust) 47
        Overwhelming Sadness 49
        Overwhelming Shock (Related to Surprise) 50
        Overwhelming Joy 52
        Summary 55

- Step 2: I. - Imitate A Relaxed Body State 56
  - 2-to-1 Breath 59
  - Relaxed posture 59
    - Summary 66
- Step 3: D - Deploy Self-Compassion 68
  - Self-Compassionate Perspective Technique 70
    - Summary 74
- Step 4: E – Evoke Connection 76
  - Evoking Connection Technique 78
    - Summary 81
- R.I.D.E. In Practise 83
  - Summary 86
- What Successful Emotional Control Looks Like 87
  - Emotional Mastery - LEVEL 1 89
  - Emotional Mastery - LEVEL 2 90
  - Emotional Mastery - LEVEL 3 92
  - Other Levels of Progress 93
    - Summary 94
- How to Make R.I.D.E. a Habit 96
  - #1 Work with Your Cue (Trigger) 100
  - Eliminate 100
  - Prepare 102
  - #2 Make it Easy to Insert a New Response (Behaviour) 104
  - #3 Find a Better Reward (Motivation) 107
    - Summary 109
- What We Can and Cannot Change 111
  - Genetics 113
  - Cultural and Social Influences 113
  - Life Circumstances 114
    - Summary 115

Final note	116
Summaries	119
About me	124
Table of Figures	126
Endnotes	127

INTRODUCTION

It is precisely the most subjective ideas which, being closer to nature and to the living being, deserve to be called the truest.

- C.C. Jung, Modern Man in Search for a Soul

It was an unflattering '360 review' – anonymous feedback process at work – that put me on the road to this book. All the 'points of improvement' indicated my inability to manage my frustrations in a calmer, less visible, and more work-appropriate way.

It didn't come as a surprise. I have been at war with my emotions all my life. When I wasn't trying to suppress my anger about a colleague's disrespectful comment or holding back tears after critical feedback, I was hyperventilating before an important meeting or hiding in shame over a spilled coffee. On top of overwhelming emotions, I often felt guilt about unleashing my anger on others, shame about my tears, or self-hatred for being so weak.

Inability to manage emotional reactions and behaviours is not just a minor inconvenience — it has real implications in professional and personal life. Emotional behaviours are most punished in the workplace, where even the smallest show of emotion can set back your career, prevent promotion, and impact your earning capacity. While emotional expressions are more accepted in relationships, the impact of emotionally driven behaviours in personal life can be even more devastating.

Dating? No dating profile includes 'drama queen,' 'hot temper,' or 'cry baby' as a desirable quality. In a relationship? No partner wants to be the recipient of your overreactions. Want to make friends? True friendships can withstand good and bad times, but behaviours like snapping or crying uncontrollably can put a major strain on – or even break – them. The impact on relationships can be so nuanced we barely notice, but it's there. Without awareness, the emotional language between partners can be misinterpreted, erode trust, and breed resentment.

When we are emotionally overwhelmed, our reactions and behaviours give away information about what's important to us — triggers, values, goals. That is normal. Communication is one of the core functions of emotions. Unfortunately, there are always people — a minority, but a toxic one — willing to exploit this information for their benefit. Even those that don't are not keen to be the recipient of that information. One person's emotions can quickly become a burden to others. Have you ever tried sitting next to a person in a foul mood and managed to stay positive?

Learning to manage your emotions is a crucial life skill — if not to save relationships or careers, at least to improve your own emotional safety.

Having experienced first-hand the destruction of emotional behaviour, I didn't need convincing I needed help.

During my '360 review' session, I immediately asked the HR Advisor — how? How do we get to that mystical place where I am calm and collected and don't take things personally or unload my emotions on others?

At first, we discussed the three most common solutions suggested to people who struggle with emotions. I now call them the Fallacy Trio - the Fallacy of Just Breathe, the Fallacy of the Root Cause, and the Fallacy of Suck it Up.

Out of the three, the Fallacy of Just Breathe is the most annoying. Anyone who ever got caught in the heat of emotions knows how impossible it feels to stop yourself from reacting, no matter whether it's anger, tears, or the urge to hide from shame. While deep breathing in a tense situation helps by stimulating our vagus nerve and calming down our nervous system[1], 'just breathe' is not a powerful enough solution.

Emotional reactions are full system responses that include 'physiological reactions, changes in both body chemistry and body language, and thoughts, triggering images, memories, and action urges as well as the actual feeling we are experiencing'[2]. Controlling any emotional reaction — let alone emotional overwhelm — means fighting your physiology (flushed cheeks, hunched shoulders, adrenaline, and cortisol flow), thoughts (memories of the similar situations, beliefs), emotions, urges, and desires. Another hundred things we don't even think of, like being thirsty or sleep-deprived, can also impact our ability to calm down. Saying 'just breathe' is like giving a knife to a soldier in a battle against drones and tanks and expecting him to come back victorious.

The Fallacy of the Root Cause is the most appealing. It assumes that if we only knew what triggers us and why, we would stop our behaviour. It's the equivalent of the fairy godmother's magic on Cinderella's appearance — as if a real-world Cinderella wouldn't have spent hours doing makeup and hair, shopping for the pair of shoes just right to drop for the Prince Charming, and then getting stuck in traffic on the way to the Most Talked About Ball in Town. Many things can go wrong in the search for the Root Cause. For one, healing requires mental health professionals to guide us through pain, memories, and emotional needs. Even when we are guided, understanding doesn't automatically bring acceptance and change. Our emotional reactions are not linear, not neatly organized occurrences that can be 'hacked.' Just like knowing that we should eat less to lose weight doesn't stop overeating, knowing our triggers doesn't stop emotional behaviour.

At any point in time, we can be impacted by hundreds if not thousands of things. Trying to untangle such a web for every emotionally tense situation is a pointless exercise. For example, I have a habit of getting angry quickly and unleashing it. It could be related to my past trauma, like bullying I experienced at school. But it could also be related to my experiences growing up, e.g., showing anger was normal in my family. It could also be connected to my personality — I am quick to anger because I am also quick to walk, think, eat, and talk. Most likely, it's all the above and more. It would be easy to point to bullying as the 'root cause,' but it's unlikely to fully explain my behaviour, nor help change it.

And finally, the Fallacy of the Suck it Up. The most popular. It's the most popular emotional management strategy in the world as we start at the cradle and never stop. If I got a dollar for every time I was told 'don't be so sensitive' or 'don't take this personally,' I would be a millionaire. As our emotions are often interpreted as weaknesses or flaws, we learn to hide them from a young age. The environment signals that the only acceptable options with emotions are to fight, flee, or freeze them, or as I call it 'Suck It Up.' The problem with these strategies is that they only work short-term without serious consequences on our wellbeing. Numb your anger, fear, or shame for too long, and you will numb your ability to feel joy, excitement, and love. Keep suppressing your emotions through willpower and you start breaking when the stress becomes too much. Avoid your emotions long enough, and you will lose depth and authenticity in your relationships or the ability to problem-solve in real-life.

I call these fallacies because they assume that if we only tried more, we would be able to stop ourselves from reacting emotionally. They assume that if only we remembered to breathe on time, knew the cause behind the trigger, or had stronger willpower, all would be well. If that is the case, what sort of conclusions can we draw when — not if — we fail? We would have to conclude that there is something wrong with us or that we haven't tried enough — and that is the biggest fallacy of all.

In the past, I had moments when I would have surgically removed my emotions, had I had that choice. Being hard on ourselves when we fail isn't just unhelpful; it can weaken our resolve to do better next time[3].

After my HR advisor and I put the fallacies aside as previously ineffective or even harmful, we arrived at our final destination. My HR advisor kindly suggested 'creating the space between the stimulus and response to choose a better behaviour.'

Ever since, I have heard this advice reiterated in many sources. It is backed by evidence to help reduce emotional reactivity and is associated with long-term mental wellbeing. The variations of this advice are plenty. Mark Brackett, the Director of Yale's Centre of Emotional Intelligence, advises the 'Meta-pause.' Dr. Joan Rosenberg, the author of *90 Seconds to a Life You Love: How to Master Your Difficult Feelings to Cultivate Lasting Confidence, Resilience, and Authenticity*, suggests to 'ride the emotional wave' for the 90 seconds in order to release the physiological reaction of the emotion out of our bodies. In *Emotional Agility: Get Unstuck, Embrace Change, and Thrive in Work and Life*, Susan Davis suggests 'stepping back' to remember our values as the key to mastering emotions.

These authors champion the more open, progressive approach to emotions and are my personal heroes. They helped me raise my self-awareness and accept my emotions as a useful part of myself. They put the emotions back where they always belonged — in our daily lives, not just behind closed doors and on therapists' couches.

Still, emotional overwhelm has unique characteristics that make 'creating the space' in the midst of it very tricky. For one, it is very quick: when we are faced with an unexpected threat, automated responses can overtake our whole body and mind, making us react without thinking. This often makes mind-based tools futile as we remember our values and long-term goals too late. Secondly, emotional overwhelm can be so intense, and can accelerate so quickly that even when we put a break between our trigger and behaviour, it often doesn't last. Finally, the social aspect of an emotionally heated situation means that we often need to react much faster than our physiological and mental reactions allow. For example, in an argument, we need to formulate an adequate response within seconds, so waiting until our anger subsides — even for 90 seconds — might not be an option. Even using the breath to calm down without others noticing can be hard. Many other tools often advised for emotional control are completely inappropriate for social situations. How often are we able to stop the meeting for a meditation break or a few push-ups?

Above all, using logic and reason to 'create the space' in the midst of emotional overwhelm takes an enormous amount of mental energy. You might have noticed that after an emotional situation, you shake out of anger, feel exhausted after tears, or feel empty after a panic attack. If we successfully suppress our response in the moment, we often express it later, such as by kicking inanimate objects or sobbing uncontrollably on the floor at home.

No — to successfully 'create the space' between our triggers and behaviours, to keep that space long enough and leave it on our terms, we need something as powerful and quick as the negative emotions that overtake us.

We need positive emotions.

Inviting emotion into an emotional situation may seem counter-intuitive, or even outrageous, but it is actually common sense. Think about it: for financial problems, we seek financial advisors; for health problems, we seek doctors. And yet for emotional issues, we overwhelmingly rely on our ability to think rather than our ability to feel. However, while our thoughts, mindset, approach, and values do help us find direction, it is often emotions that fuel us towards it: feelings, such as the joy of friendships, excitement over challenges, or pride about achievements.

We may think that this tendency of emotion for action is what gets us into trouble. But it can help too! Recently, more robust research has started to confirm what I've known intuitively all my life: Emotions are not just a force of destruction; Emotions actually can power us towards our goals. In his book *Emotional Success: The Power of Gratitude, Passion, and Pride*, David DeSteno builds an elegant and robust case for using our emotions to increase our chances of success in life.

Based on research, practise, and my own successes (and failures), I built a 4-step tool for emotionally intense situations that utilizes the power of emotions, rather than fighting it. It's called R.I.D.E.

R.

Recognize the physiological and mental signs of emotional overwhelm, prompting us to start 'creating the space.'

I.

Imitate the relaxed state to win a few seconds, even in the midst of the overwhelm, gaining some time to switch emotional gears.

D.

Deploy self-compassion during emotional moments.

E.

Evoke connection with others in the emotional situation, to move from an overwhelming negative emotion to a genuinely positive one — compassion.

R.I.D.E. helps not only to 'create that space' but also to leave that space on your own terms through the power of positive emotions. It is a full-system solution to a full-system reaction rather than reliance only on willpower, reason, or body. I chose actions in R.I.D.E. that can be deployed quickly and subtly to maximize the chances of 'creating the space' in a heated moment.

R.I.D.E. is unashamedly and proudly a self-help tool. It is not a replacement for treatment of mental illness or trauma, but something to help with emotional overwhelm in daily situations. While it doesn't solve any underlying issues behind emotionally driven behaviours, it helps you manage your emotions in difficult moments.

The lack of how-to that existed before R.I.D.E. was a compelling enough reason for me to write this book. As someone who is not a scientist, therapist, psychologist, or a spiritual leader, I had major reservations about advising people. However, precisely because I found it extremely difficult to find advice about emotional control that didn't numb me, stress me, or exhaust me – advice that evoked a demand to change almost everything who I am – I realized it also might be helpful to others.

'Treat the disease, not the symptom,' they say. As someone who has an autoimmune disease with no clear cause, I must say this advice is a luxury for those who exactly what the 'disease' is. 'Do what you can, with what you've got, and where you are' is actually the advice I have found more useful in my life, from nobody less than 26th U.S. President Theodore Roosevelt. Sometimes advice about *how* to keep going is more important than understanding everything about the *why* of what's happening.

I might not know the '*why*', but I know the '*how*' because I deal with emotional overwhelm almost every day. I know how it feels when you might 'lose it' at any time. I've lost my temper more times than I can count, leaving destruction, shattered relationships, and people hurt along the way. I've cried in front of bosses, in meetings, and in front of big audiences. I've hyperventilated or had full-blown panic attacks in social and professional situations.

I found some answers about the '*why*' in Dr. Elaine Aaron's work on Highly Sensitive Persons (HSPs). Hypersensitivity is a physiological trait of up to 20% of the population, also observed in many other species. HSPs have a hyperactive nervous system that can be easily overwhelmed as it is more attuned to the environment. Also, or perhaps as a consequence, many HSPs absorb an unhealthy amount of other people's emotions and are sometimes referred to as 'empaths' or as having a 'highly altruistic' trait.

Some HSPs internalize their daily emotional overwhelm by shying away from noisy environments, reducing their exposure to triggers, and removing themselves from certain situations to work through their emotions in private. Others deal with overwhelm by externalizing it — releasing emotions on to others or talking about them with others.

I'm not sure how I chose to externalize as my go-to strategy, but I know exactly how much it hurts me. Internalizing emotional overwhelm can have a serious impact on physical and mental health. But, in my experience, externalizing emotional overwhelm is arguably worse because external reactions are highly visible, often exposing me to emotional exploitation or overburdening people around me.

Carl Jung, in the book *'Modern Man in Search for a Soul'* teaches us that our subjective ideas can be the truest because they are the closest to us. And there is no one closer to the problem of emotional overwhelm than an HSP. The hyperactive system, absorption of others' emotions, and living daily with the destructive impact of emotional behaviour ensures that HSPs have a front seat in understanding emotional overwhelm.

Since I started working *with* emotions instead of fighting them, I fended off panic attacks, stopped before losing my temper, proactively managed paralyzing grief, and forgot what overwhelming embarrassment looks like. While I still get myself into heated arguments (not everything can or should be changed) my blow-ups are rarer and milder. Ironically, I've become so skilled at R.I.D.E. that I only 'lose it' when I am caught off guard, i.e., in an emotionally safe environment. While it's not ideal, as my closest circle suffers the most from my emotional reactions, fortunately these people are also most likely to understand and tolerate such behaviour. The fact that I can avoid this is most personal and professional situations is a clear sign of success: the luxury of forgetting to manage yourself is only earned through daily experiences of emotional mastery.

As a nice bonus, I also rarely feel bad or weak. Taking guilt trips and feeling shame after emotional behaviour is no fun.

R.I.D.E. helps avoid them altogether. Not only is it a nicer way to live, it positively impacts my mental and physical health by helping me avoid the destructive impact of anger. Did you know that being prone to anger can significantly increase the chance of a heart attack[4]?

It is the massive increase in energy, however, that I enjoy the most. By changing my approach to emotions, I save the energy that otherwise would be wasted to fight them. Given the crazy pace of modern life, additional energy is life changing.

But this book is not built on success — it is built on failure. It is only because I failed that I now know 'count to 10' is not strong enough to pull me out of emotionally-driven behaviours. It is only because I failed that I know I snap the 5th time when rudely interrupted, not the first, second, or third. It is only because I failed that I know how bad it feels when your emotions are used against you or the sheer exhaustion from fighting emotions all day.

I wrote this book because I was tired. Tired of feeling helpless against my reactions. Tired of feeling guilty, ashamed, or judged by my emotionally driven behaviours. But most of all, I was tired of all the well-meaning but not-good-enough advice offered to 'help' me.

So, you keep finding yourself losing control again and again. You're sick of being labelled a drama queen or a sensitive flower. You want to stop bleeding friends or career opportunities. Or maybe you are sick of feeling numb, exhausted, or fake from suppressing your emotions, you might think to yourself: there must be a better way!

You know what? There is.

SECTION I - INTRODUCTION TO EMOTIONAL HIJACKING & THE R.I.D.E. PROCESS

HOW DO WE GET EMOTIONALLY OVERWHELMED?

We think of ourselves as thinking creatures who think, but biologically, we are feeling creatures who think.

- Jill Bolte Taylor, My Stroke of Insight

It's July 9, 2006, and emotions are running high on the soccer field in Olympiastadion, Berlin. The FIFA World Cup Final between Italy and France — rivals in both history and football — is in full swing, with 715 million people watching. As expected, the game is an emotional rollercoaster. Zinedine Zidane, affectionately called Zizou, scores the first goal after a questionable penalty. His soon-to-be nemesis Marco Materazzi scores soon after. Both teams have more chances to score. One goal is nullified after a controversial offside; another near-miss is a controversial behaviour not punished by a penalty kick.

The game ends in a draw, 1-1. After a short break, footballers come back for a 30-minute extension. Zidane kicks a hopeful one to the gate, only for it to be brilliantly saved by the Italian goalkeeper.

Five minutes after the unsuccessful kick, Zidane is jogging alongside Marco. They briefly exchange words. Marco even pulls Zidane's t-shirt. Doing his best to ignore Marco, Zidane pulls away while Marco keeps muttering insults under his breath. What happens next will go down in sports history. Zidane turns back and shoves his head into Marco's chest with great force, pushing him to the ground. He gets the red card and leaves the field.

During the penalty shootout, Italy wins the World Cup.

Did I mention that this was the last game of Zidane's career?

It was a thriller for the spectators but a tragedy for one of football's greatest. Zizou's passion and talent inspired a whole new generation of footballers. If you don't know who Zidane is, imagine Roger Federer finishing his career by throwing a tennis racket at Djokovic or Tom Brady finishing his American NFL career by getting into a brawl with a referee.

Zidane's headbutt is one of the most famous episodes of something called **amygdala hijacking.** It's a process that includes part of the brain's limbic system called the amygdala responding to a threat without consulting the slower, more perspective-taking parts of the brain. The amygdala's reaction protects us from dangers, making us react without thinking to save our lives, but it is not always accurate and can mistake a minor threat for a big one, making us behave in ways that we regret later.

Amygdala Hijacking

In 2008, George W. Bush, then President of the United States, was holding a press conference when a member of the audience threw a shoe at him. The President ducked so quickly that the shoe flew over his head without touching him, prompting commentators to marvel at his incredible reaction.

That is a classic case of amygdala hijacking — a reaction to the imminent threat that happens so fast that you act without thinking.

If you don't have shoes thrown at you often, you might have jumped off the street if the car was fast approaching or slammed on the brakes when somebody cut you off on the road. Your body reacted so quickly that you were safe even before you realized there was a threat. In both situations, you did not have time to contemplate the best course of action. Engaging the more sophisticated but slower parts of the brain might have costed you your life.

The amygdala sits in a part of the brain called the limbic system, which is the brain's emotional centre, impacting our learning and memory. The amygdala's strategic position, roughly where your eye and ears meet, could explain how it can bypass the rest of the brain. As it receives signals of danger from either your eyes or ears, it can act fast and mobilize your body to act without thinking. Notably, the amygdala seems to only *react in ways it responded in the past*, prioritizing speed over quality to get you to safety. This might be why our emotional reactions feel so repetitive. They often come from previously-stored memories.

The physiology of amygdala hijacking is fast and powerful. As mentioned before, any emotional reaction is a full system response. The physiological aspects might last from 6 seconds[5] to 40-50[6] or even 90 seconds[7]. Amygdala hijacking, however, seems to be stronger and last longer. It can take only milliseconds to gear for response and hours for the stress hormone cortisol to clear from our bodies.

Remember the last time you had a road incident. Did you start shouting at the other driver who could neither hear you nor undo his action? Did you sulk about it for hours after? If you did, you are not alone. In one U.S. study, nearly 78% of participants admitted to aggressive behaviour on the road, e.g., futile yelling (47%), honking (45%), and making angry gestures (33%[8]).

There is a reason why road incidents can overwhelm us so much. They are arguably one of the few remaining life-threatening situations in modern society. As for the rest of our lives, amygdala hijacking is redundant. However, instead of retreating, it sends its first cousin - emotional overwhelm - to fight the battles of modern life.

Emotional Overwhelm vs. Amygdala Hijacking

Road incidents or an occasional disease aside, our survival and success in modern society are almost exclusively defined by our social connections both professional and personal. As such, the only threats we face are social. Social responses don't require the full-blow amygdala hijacking. What we need are more nuanced, tamed, and complex reactions, more appropriate for lower-level threats.

And yet evolution – which sculpted our bodies and minds for survival over millions of years – moves at a snail's pace. Just as our bodies have not adjusted to the modern diet or sitting so much at the office, we seem to be slow to switch from life-or-death responses to more appropriate ones.

You don't need to look far for examples. We know that neither honking nor rude gestures help us on the road. Nor does losing your temper at a colleague, tearing up in front of your boss, or storming out of a room over a spilled drink help you at work. Still, our bodies respond as if we are in danger - in the same ways that the amygdala reacted thousands of years ago. No wonder 'just breathe' isn't strong enough!

The good news is that our brains seem to already know there is a difference between life-or-death and social threats. Amygdala hijacking in the case of social threats seems to take time to interpret the situation so it's slower and at least partially, conscious. We might curl our hands into fists when we are angry, but we rarely actually punch. The time difference is also significant. George W. Bush took less than a second to duck while Zidane took 11 seconds to walk angrily and headbutt Marco.

While amygdala hijacking explains a lot about our emotionally-driven behaviours, the differences in time and level of interpretation involved in the case of social threats are significant. To note this difference, I call the socially-driven amygdala responses emotional overwhelm. I'm referring to the reactions powerful enough to overwhelm our bodies and minds near completely and yet not so fast that we shouldn't try and stop it.

Emotional Overwhelm Characteristics

While we rarely think of it this way, every day is an emotional rollercoaster. Before 10 a.m., we may get frustrated about being late, angry about someone cutting us off in the line for coffee, stressed about driving in traffic, and embarrassed when a colleague doesn't respond to a friendly hello. It is just a matter of time until some of those emotions boil over and make us behave in ways we may regret. Often, this happens at the least opportune time.

Since fast reactions tap into the pool of previous situations, responses, and memories, our behaviour often repeats again and again, making us feel stuck. While repetition might be annoying, recognizing those repetitive patterns can work in our favour. We can recognise our patterns in time and change them.

The core characteristics of the emotional overwhelm are:

1. **Intensity.** Before and during it, you feel it in:
    a **Body.** Heat in the head, tense pose, strong urge to respond physically, with a punch, a yell, a cry, or an urgent desire to run away.
    b. **Mind**. Ability to think is significantly impaired. Often, we experience a sensation of the mind going blank. Our communication is also in trouble — therefore 'think before you act' doesn't work.
2. **Briefness.** The typical emotional reaction is a biochemical signal in your brain that lasts up to 90 seconds. While some bodily responses, like stress hormones, can take a few hours to clear out, your emotionally-driven

behaviours, overreactions, and responses are likely to be over quickly.

3. **Destructiveness**. You don't need to finish your career with 715 million people watching to know the destructive power of emotional behaviour. You might have lost friends, soured, or ruined work relationships, or undermined your career. You might not even know the full impact of your emotional behaviour on your health – for example, frequent displays of anger were linked to higher chance of heart attacks in some studies.

The R.I.D.E tool recognizes those repetitive patterns, taps into them to mobilize the equally strong power of positive emotions, and stops the reaction on time. In the next chapter, you will learn the R.I.D.E. process and how it can help you stop feeling out of control and at the mercy of your own emotions.

Summary

1. Amygdala hijacking is a process that bypasses the slower, perspective-taking parts of the brain to respond quickly and ensure our survival.

2. Modern life has much fewer external threats but many more social ones. These social threats are more complex and take longer to resolve, giving us time to formulate better responses.

3. 'Emotional hijacking' explains why it is so hard to stop ourselves in the midst of a heated moment, but 'emotional overwhelm' better captures the slower, tamer reaction that better suits social threats.

R.I.D.E. - FOUR STEPS OUT OF EMOTIONAL OVERWHELM

You gotta fight drama with drama.

- Gina Linetti, Brooklyn 99

As a professional athlete, Zidane probably got access to the best sports coaching in the world. He probably had perfectly tailored nutritional and body training programs to be at the top of his form. He probably spent hours mentally preparing for crowds' booing or cheers and had played hundreds of frustrating, intense, and successful games.

So how can a verbal insult about someone who wasn't even there take a professional athlete out of the most important game of his life?

It wasn't just an insult. Zidane was probably physically exhausted after 100 minutes of gameplay, frustrated by missed chances to score, and mentally exhausted from pressure to win. He was perhaps vulnerable — sad, anxious, or joyful — about the last minutes of his career ticking away.

This is how real life works. We rarely snap the first time someone interrupts or insults us — we snap after a night of poor sleep, a frustrating encounter on the way to work, or receiving bad news. Things we don't even think about, like being thirsty[9] or hungry[10], can strongly impact our emotional state, usually increasing our anxiety and negativity.

We lose control when we are overwhelmed, and it is when we are overwhelmed that our tools to control ourselves fail the fastest. **Since we rely on our minds for so much during the day — planning, thinking, making judgements, communicating thoughts — it is no wonder that when we also ask our minds to battle our bodies and emotions, it so often fails.**

R.I.D.E. not only recognizes this interconnectedness of our minds, bodies, and multi-layered pressures; it also deploys our bodies, emotions, and minds to help us cope. R.I.D.E. also acknowledges the reality of social pressures — their diversity and social aspects — and can be deployed across various situations. Zidane would never be allowed to pause for a moment of peace to meditate or do alternate nostril breathing to calm down, so other options are needed.

There is one obstacle that stands in a way of deploying R.I.D.E, though.

Let me take you on a small detour. Imagine you have severe pain in your stomach and get an urgent appointment with your doctor. Who do you think has more information to help you with pain — you or her? You might assume it's the doctor. If not, why are you there? However, short of giving you a morphine injection, the doctor is nearly helpless unless she knows when the pain started, its exact location, whether you felt it before, whether it's increasing or reducing over time, and so on. The more information about your body and its signals you give, the better she can help. The reasons for pain are far from obvious. A sleepless night, stress at work, or other medication can impact them, none of which a doctor knows without you. Despite so much of our body state and information depending on us, most of us barely register this information and can only stammer, 'My tummy hurts.'

The fact that we may be able to blurt out the exact amount of proteins we need per day but can't explain our bodily sensations any better than a 4-year-old is bad enough; still worse is having even less awareness of our thoughts and emotions. We marvel at how our brains are capable of amazing inventions but are completely unaware that we sulk for half a day about a minor comment from the boss. While we barely notice our thoughts, we flatly deny our emotions, treating them as a nuisance or something 'to get over.'

This lack of self-awareness and invalidation of our inner worlds often stands between you and change.

And this is what **Step 1** overcomes.

Step 1. R. – **R**ecognize the signs.

GOAL: Recognize the signs of emotional hijacking early enough to change the course of your behaviour.

In a clear-cut amygdala hijacking — a life-or-death event — preventing automatic reaction is neither possible nor desirable. In the case of social threats, on the other hand, we have just enough time to notice the physical changes in our body. When we have a strong urge to cry, our voices get wobbly, and our eyes may tingle. We may get tense when angry or play with our arms when anxious. Those signs are like canaries in the mines that warn about the upcoming disaster.

In **Step 1**, you learn to capture the signs of your emotional overwhelm by using the **Triangle Tool** that captures your personal **Emotional Footprint**. I included a sample **Emotional Footprint** for each of the six basic emotions felt by humans near-universally, but it can also be used with other emotions that trigger our emotionally-driven responses.

Capturing your body and mind signals gives you a chance to insert better and more powerful tools to counter your emotional overwhelm. However, awareness is not the same as action, just its enabler. To counter something as powerful as emotional overwhelm, you need something more.

What you need is more time.

Step 2. I. – Imitate a relaxed state.

GOAL: Give yourself time to determine a better response by slowing down your body's reaction to emotional overwhelm.

During emotional overwhelm, the body releases a lot of energy, either to prepare us for a threat or to communicate our emotion to others. Anger posture makes our body look taller in preparation for a fight. Fear sends blood pumping to our legs to flee. Slumped shoulders when we feel sad communicate retreat, asking others to take care of us or at least not expect much from us while we grieve. This amount of energy is powerful. That's why self-control feels so impossible in a heated moment. Instead of fighting this energy, we can switch body gears from a stress-based bodily response to a more relaxed state with the help of deep breathing and posture change.

Step 2 is about imitating the most relaxed state you can imagine, then deploying it in the heat of the moment, without looking unprofessional or needing a lot of time. You do have to be careful about what relaxed state you choose, of course: I don't suggest lying down in the middle of an argument. Once you imagine a reasonably relaxed position with vivid details (e.g. shoulders and hands relaxed, neck and spine pulling back), you can practice it and store it in your memory to access later.

The good news is that achieving even half-success in imitating a relaxed state is often enough to control yourself as long as necessary for the incident. Even a few seconds won in the heat of the moment gives you a much better chance to leave the situation on your own terms.

To truly calm down, however, you will need stronger tools than just body. At this point, engaging willpower or pushing your emotions away will also be easier, because you have already switched gears. But rarely does suppression of emotions help manage emotions in a way that doesn't have a related negative impact. *Engaging* our emotions in emotionally intense situations is healthier, and more sustainable as a long-term way to control ourselves.

Step 3 and **4** are about how to invite *compassion* — first to yourself, and then to others — to counter your overwhelming anger, shame, fear, or sadness.

Step 3. D. – **D**eploy self-compassion.

GOAL: Reduce negative emotional overwhelm with a positive emotion.

Imagine yourself in the middle of an argument, where you feel strong frustration about your project lagging due to other people. Suddenly, your opponent stops and says: 'I understand you are angry; you have a right to feel this way.' How do you think you would feel? Chances are that such an acknowledgment of your perspective might at least result in a diminishment of your emotional intensity, and at best, it might even end the argument. Could direct confrontation be avoided if you just had that moment to feel heard and respected? Of course, we cannot always depend on others to offer us that kind attention in a heated moment. But we are always able to give it to ourselves, and that can have its own powerful effect.

Step 3 utilises the power of emotions — in this case, *compassion* — by making that power work for us, not against us. Instead of fighting against or trying to avoid our emotions (which often comes at a terrible cost, resulting in everything from a ruined day, mental breakdowns, or an impact on our personal life), we invite a positive emotion of *compassion* to counter the negative ones.

To be clear, other emotions could do the job too - compassion towards self is simply easier to deploy on short notice than, say, gratitude.

Kindness towards yourself when you're in the midst of pain is powerful. It's like having your best friend nearby, validating your feelings and showing unquestioned support in the exact moment of pain. There is plenty of research confirming that compassion and kindness can bring health benefits, improve relationships, increase longevity, and boost our mental and physical performance. (Yes, you heard right. Emotions don't just hinder but help even professional athletes.) Compassion has also been proven to reduce aggression and control anger, the strongest and arguably the most destructive emotion for social situations. Importantly, inviting positive emotions — any positive emotions — broadens our thinking[11] and encourages prosocial behaviour[12].

In addition, you can boost the power of self-compassion by deploying it together with another tool that has been proven to reduce emotional overwhelm - a 'third-person' technique. In your mind you can address yourself, even by name, as though you are a third person present in the incident. This creates a kind of emotional distance, even for a few seconds, that can take the intensity out of a difficult encounter. Physically stepping away may not be possible or appropriate, but we can let our mind give us space. In the heated moment, stepping away is both the best and the hardest thing to do. Just saying your own name to yourself, followed by a word or phrase of encouragement, can help distance you from the situation for a moment without consuming a lot of mental energy.

Step 3 teaches us to be kind to ourselves and reduce the emotional intensity of an emotionally charged situation. It also is a step towards compassion for others. We are reminding ourselves that often we all feel the same. We build on commonalities and not differences with other people.

This is what **Step 4** is about.

Step 4. E. – Evoke connection

GOAL: Get back in control of your emotion by seeking commonality, not differences.

Compassion connects. Finding connection with people around you in an emotionally charged situation helps you see them more like kin, like a fellow human, and less of an opponent or enemy.

Most social triggers include other people and evoking connection with them makes it easier to see your criticizing boss as someone who also cares about team results instead of just a prick. Or see your mother-in-law as someone who cares about her son instead of a bully. And a fellow football player as someone who loves winning as much as you do, not just a jerk.

You can **evoke connection** in many ways. Even the smallest connection counts. You might have children who are the same age or like the same brand of beer. Finding something that links you with another person invites compassion if not about the person's behaviour, then about the person him- or herself. Connection invites compassion and compassion reduces the intensity of negative feelings in the midst of emotional overwhelm.

Compassion has the power to get you out of the grip of negative emotion entirely rather than postponing your emotional reaction until another thought ('what a jerk') or trigger (a scoff on top of a critical remark) comes. Compassion is your way out, on your own terms.

R.I.D.E. accepts the realities of emotional overwhelm — the social aspects of it, the interconnectedness of our minds and bodies, and the power of negative emotions. Instead of fighting those realities or emotions, R.I.D.E. engages your full self to find the way out of the emotional situation without negative consequences. Since it can be mobilized within seconds, it gives you enough time to get back in the driver's seat. By deploying compassion — first for yourself, second, to others - R.I.D.E. helps you mobilize the power of positive emotion to pull yourself out of emotionally charged situations.

Before launching into details about how to practise R.I.D.E., there are a few common traps to watch out for. This is what next chapter is about.

Summary

1. To successfully change your behaviour in an emotionally charged situation, you need to know your body's signs and learn to read them to prevent behavioural disasters.

2. R.I.D.E. lies on the assumption that your body, thoughts, and emotions are valuable sources of information that you can apply to master self-control in a healthier and genuinely lasting way, rather than suppression of, avoidance of, or distraction from your emotions.

3. The power of R.I.D.E. rides in using positive emotions to counter negative ones, instead of fighting them. Positive emotions broaden our view, reduce emotional intensity, and encourage prosocial behaviours, all of which helps us to pull out of the situation that is dominated by negative, intense emotions, pre-conscious thoughts and urges, and anti-social behaviours.

BE AWARE OF THESE THREE TRAPS

Every day you must unlearn the ways that hold you back.

- Leon Brown

Just before the incident, you can see Zidane taking some time before the headbutting of Marco - about 11 seconds, to be exact. He has 11 seconds to stop himself before erupting and a lifetime afterward to apologize and make it right.

And yet Zidane never made it right. Long after the incident, he defended his reaction, saying that Marco deserved what he got because of what he said. I feel his pain. When a bully harasses, hurts, and disrespects others and gets to walk away unscathed or even undisturbed, I get caught up in the unfairness, too.

And yet, this sort of thinking is a trap — a dangerous one.

Trap #1. Being a Victim

Regardless of the situation, letting someone make you feel a certain way is giving them power over you.

No matter how unfair the situation is, the social and interconnected world we live in means that it is our responsibility to manage our reactions to whatever is going on around us. While there are situations that need pushback, standing up for ourselves, or showing emotion, it is rare that a situation warrants the intensity of amygdala hijacking. Our ability to balance our reactions — stay calm under social pressure, manage stresses without being overwhelmed, and do this daily — defines our success and upward mobility in a modern society. **As such, no matter how hard the circumstances or justified the reasons behind the triggers, our reactions are ours to manage.** Anything else is just being a victim.

A victim trap can lead to another type of trap.

Trap #2. I am right, and he is wrong

One can waste years and decades trying to be right. Zinedine Zidane, to this day, is adamant that his opponent had no right to say what he said. At the same time, Marco Materazzi is adamant that no matter how stupid his remark was, such a violent response was unwarranted.

While trying to prove our truths, we forget that there is no such thing as one reality. Our emotions, thoughts, beliefs, cultural backgrounds, and temperaments colour how we see things, exercise judgment, and define our values. In a way, every person lives their own unique reality.

Arguing about who is righter is an unwinnable situation and can go in circles indefinitely. **Only one thing that truly matters when judging our actions and behaviours: Do they leave us better or worse?**

It is fair to say that Zidane was left much worse. Without its key player, the French team lost the World Cup and Zidane was forced out of the last minutes of his career. Even leaving with the best player's award, he could not wash the taint of the incident.

I can only guess, but leaving the field at the height of emotional overwhelm might have left Zidane in one more trap.

Trap #3. I shouldn't be feeling this way

While not often mentioned, there is another trap that often awaits us after an emotionally intense situation: the feelings about feelings. We grow up hearing that our minds are extraordinary while emotions are shameful or primitive, so we start internalizing them very early. Unwittingly, this creates another layer of suffering because when we feel something, we think we are weak or inadequate because of it.

Emotions are a big part of being human. It doesn't mean we should express everything we feel, but emotions, even overwhelming ones, are neither good nor bad. They are simply information about our internal state. **Emotions don't define us. Just because we get overwhelmed by anger sometimes, doesn't define us as an angry person. Just because we feel something doesn't make us a weakling.**

Sometimes learning the new is about unlearning the old, and those three traps are worth unlearning.

If you're still hung up about the unfairness, remember that life has its way of settling the scores. Even though Zinedine Zidane finished his career condemned for violent behaviour, Marco Materazzi spent years proving he was not just a provocateur, but also a good football player. The incident overshadowed his career so much that he wrote a book ten years later. He said, 'I do not understand why this story reached such large proportions. The only thing I want to remember about me is my two goals in the final.'

In a way, being remembered for being headbutted rather than his skill is his penance.

Summary

1. Decades can be lost on unwinnable arguments, proving subjective truths, or pointing fingers.
2. The question that matters is. 'Are your emotional responses helpful or hurtful?'
3. Life has its ways to settle scores. You don't need to do its job.

SECTION II -
R.I.D.E.: FOUR STEPS OUT OF EMOTIONAL HIJACKING

STEP 1: R. - RECOGNIZE THE SIGNS EARLY

No one likes to be over-aroused, HSP or not. A person feels out of control, and a whole body warns that it is in trouble. Over-arousal means failing to perform at one's best.

- Elaine N. Aron, The Highly Sensitive Person

Not everybody knows this, but Zidane's last game of his career was not the first time he headbutted someone during the game. For his die-hard fans, he was already known as somewhat of an angry player. In the year 2000, he headbutted an opponent during the Champions League match, and he stomped on a Saudi Arabian opponent two years earlier in the World Cup. Some even found a parallel between his edgy successful performance and his anger, noting that as Zidane reduced his rage, his game somewhat mellowed too.

Many thoughts, emotions, and behaviours we experience daily are mostly the same day in and day out. It is both good and bad. It's bad when repetitive patterns hurt us, like reaching for a cigarette when stressed, or automatically taking things personally. But it's good when we want to pick up newer, better behaviours.

Even though we can't prepare for all the intense situations in life, we can learn to notice our triggers, sensitivities, and dominant emotions to be prepared when they come.

As you probably noticed, a big part of an emotional reaction is preconscious. Do you ever find your hands curled into fists when somebody insults you? Or do you find yourself physically shrinking away from an angry person? Have you ever been around someone that made you feel unsafe?

In the video of the headbutt incident, Zidane starts going towards Materazzi and in a few seconds you can see his body gearing up for action — his walk is angry, his shoulders are ready, and his whole body is tense. Those are the signs of the body preparing for action in response to a threat.

Those few seconds might not sound like a lot but considering the amygdala response to a threat can occur in milliseconds[13], a few full seconds can make a difference. It might be too late for Zidane to save his career, but it is not too late for us to succeed in our lives.

Triangle Tool to Master R. - Recognizing Signs

The **Triangle Tool** introduced below achieves two goals. First, it helps bring self-awareness about the signals of overwhelm specific to you. Second, it helps capture those signs early enough to change the direction of emotional behaviour.

The tool captures the complex interplay between body, mind, and emotion, effectively creating the **Emotional Footprint** of overwhelm. Importantly, it captures the nuances and specifics of your emotional reaction, your triggers, your preferred expressions, and the context. Although it is widely agreed that most humans feel a handful of the same emotions, how we express them and cope with them is impacted by our past, culture, physiology, and other factors. For example, say you were accused of lying to a close friend years ago. Chances are, you still get triggered if someone questions your truthfulness. This trigger would be much more significant for you than other people. For Zidane, cultural beliefs about family and the need to protect it might have contributed to his overreaction on the field. If Marco insulted his bad performance, he might have laughed it off. **The knowledge and awareness of specific triggers maximise your chances of recognizing signs of overwhelm early**.

The most important signs to capture with the **Triangle Tool** are:

1. **Body changes** - conscious and unconscious responses
2. **Emotion** - the dominant feeling that overwhelms you
3. **Thoughts** - repetitive ideas that fuel emotion, not diffuse it

It might be worth capturing other aspects of emotional overwhelm, like triggers or faulty beliefs, in the **Triangle Tool**. This brings a broader insight into what gets you into an emotional state and work with that.

Body

Here is what to look for in your body:

1. **Sensations:**
   a. Temperature — getting cold or hot in different parts of the body
   b. Tensions — stiffness in the neck, upper back, or jaw
   c. Other feelings — tingling in the nose before you cry or the sensation of a rash forming on your back when you're anxious.
2. **Breath** — shortness of breath before an anxiety attack
3. **Involuntary movements** — grinding jaw, twisting hands, complete freeze, shaking hands, face twitches

Helpful Tool – Emotion Body Maps

Finnish scientists did excellent research that got nods from world-renowned emotion experts like Antonio Damasio. The scientists asked a group of 700 individuals from Finland, Sweden, and Taiwan to map[14] where they feel their emotions. Many participants reported remarkably similar sensations when comparing emotional states to neutral:

1. In **Anger**, participants reported strong sensations in upper body, including head, in particular strong sensations in the chest and hands.
2. When in **Fear**, the sensations were spread across the whole body, with particularly strong feelings in the chest area, consistent with fear being crowned the queen of all emotions.

Step 1: R. - Recognize the signs early

3. Interestingly, **Happiness** felt nearly as strong as fear, with participants reporting sensations across the whole body, in particular chest and head. This just confirms that whilst emotions as phenomena are universal, but the physical sensations are not very distinctive.
4. **Disgust** was reported as felt in upper body mostly, much of strongest feelings concentrating in tummy and throat area.
5. **Sadness** very much felt around the heart of most participants and belly area.
6. And finally, **Surprise** was mostly contained in the upper body, in particular head and chest area.

You can use those signals for guidance when trying to locate your own emotions, noting that you are unique, so differences can be significant.

Thoughts

While emotions and bodily sensations express themselves in similar patterns, thoughts are more specific to the situation. For example, you might feel sad due to your pet's death or because your colleague resigning. Your thoughts will be very different in each situation despite feeling the same emotion and similar bodily sensations.

When recording thoughts, capture those characteristics:

1. **The thought itself**
2. **Repetitive patterns** — like rumination, judgment, blaming others, denial

Helpful Tool - Common Repetitive Thoughts

Since so many of our thoughts feel repetitive, it is worth noting a few categories of thoughts when thinking about yours.

Researchers in the University of Kentucky mapped out the key patterns of the repetitive thinking[15] through the purpose (certain/uncertain) and valence (positive/negative) lenses. **Lack of control**, **worry**, **rumination**, **self-reproach** was deemed quite *certain* thoughts but experienced as *negative*, except for **intrusions** being *uncertain* and *negative*. On the opposite end, they found **emotional processing**, **self-analysis,** and **reflection** as quite *uncertain*, but *positively* experienced. The only thought patterns they found pleasant *and* certain, were **savouring**, **anticipating**, and **reminiscing**.

None of these thought patterns – positive or negative qualities aside– are inherently bad or good. They are qualities of our thoughts that can be helpful when considering your repetitive thought patterns and their usefulness to our goals. For example, reflection, whilst on the negative end of valence (a negative experience), is inherently useful (just remember Socrates' 'unexamined life is not worth living'). In a similar way, rumination is positive in intent, it is quite unpleasant (negative valence) and can be even harmful.

Another worthy consideration with thoughts is from 'cognitive distortions' perspective. Cognitive distortions are the filters that we often apply without noticing, that distort our interpretations of the real situation. For example, catastrophizing is about blowing the impact of one mistake out of proportion when it might not be a big deal. The common distortions are noted in the diagram below. Reviewing it might help you see if there is one that you often apply, so that you can be better prepared for it.

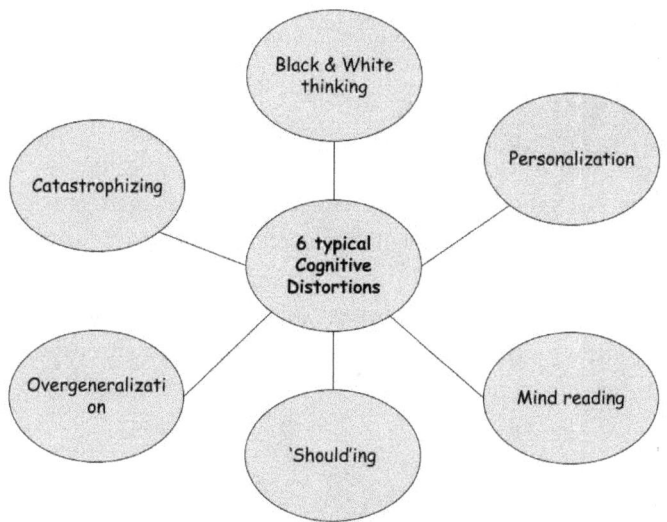

Figure 1 - 6 Typical Cognitive Distortions

Emotions

Dr. Paul Ekman identified six core emotions that are near-universally felt by humans, despite cultural and social differences in their expressions. The Six Basic Emotions Model is a useful starting point for emotional overwhelm as many intense situations can be traced back to the main six emotions.

The six core emotions are:

1. Fear
2. Anger

3. Sadness
4. Disgust
5. Surprise, and
6. Happiness.

Helpful Tool - Emotion Wheel

Below is a visual guide that captures the six basic emotions and introduces another 12 related but different intensity emotions. If you know those, you are on the way to recognizing more nuanced, synthesized emotions like longing or jealousy, which can be a mix of resentment, contempt, and sadness.

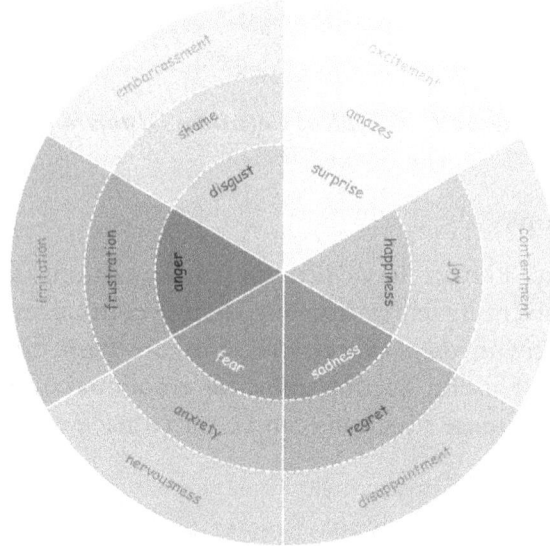

Figure 2 - Emotion Wheel

Step 1: R. - Recognize the signs early

Many of these tools will help to develop your **Emotional Footprint**, but I also prepared six case studies of emotional overwhelm as examples.

Six Case Studies of Emotional Overwhelm

These case studies include not just five negative emotions, but also one positive one. Typically, we don't need guidance for positive emotions. Remember how intoxicating your first love felt, and you will want *more* of this, not *less*. However, positive emotional overwhelm can also have unwanted consequences. For example, you might not be keen to have your greatest triumph — at work, in a sport, or in your personal life —ruined by crying and hiccups, even happiness-hiccups. Overwhelming happiness can also be unproductive. I had my worst exam results when I fell in love… No wonder, because I was so happy that I didn't hear a word my lecturers said for weeks!

Here are a few examples of overwhelming emotions.

Overwhelming Anger

Potential body signals - outbursts, rage, leashing out, yelling

Zidane's headbutt is probably a clear enough example, but if you want to see more, try searching 'Ukrainian parliament fistfight' or 'parliamentarian egged' in YouTube. A closer to home is road rage incidents that many have experienced.

As noted above, emotional overwhelm has specific characteristics, similar but not the same as amygdala hijacking:

1. It's brief (main reaction, although some signs can take hours to clear)

2. It's intense and overwhelming (body very tense, mind blank), and
3. It has a destructive impact, either externally (e.g., angry behaviours) or internally (feeling incapacitated/frozen/hopeless)

Road rage incidents tick all three boxes. They are relatively short, can feel intense, and are often quite destructive. Once, before a basketball match, my friend and I waited for 10 minutes for a parking space to become available, only for someone to swoop in and take it. Consumed by rage, I got out of the car and told the guy to move. While he obeyed, this was not my proudest moment, nor a pleasant experience. I looked like a lunatic doing that and it ruined my enjoyment of the game.

In the triangle tool below, you can see the experience captured.

Case Study - Anger

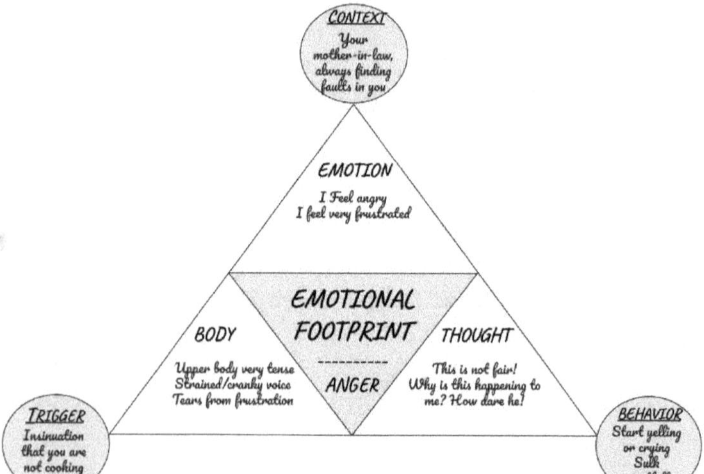

CONTEXT
Your mother-in-law, always finding faults in you

EMOTION
I feel angry
I feel very frustrated

EMOTIONAL FOOTPRINT

BODY
Upper body very tense
Strained/cranky voice
Tears from frustration

ANGER

THOUGHT
This is not fair!
Why is this happening to me? How dare he!

TRIGGER
Insinuation that you are not cooking well

BEHAVIOR
Start yelling or crying
Sulk resentfully

Figure 3 - Emotional Footprint of Anger

Ready to go deeper? Emotions are information about your internal or external state to help you survive or thrive (or both). This information sends signals about the needs you have and guides you towards satisfying them. Try reflecting. What is the need behind your overwhelming anger? It might be about undoing a wrong, the need to restore your boundaries, or the need to get past the obstacle between you and your goal. Anger might be also hiding something else. For example, you might be using anger to hide your fear.

Overwhelming Fear

Potential body signals - panic attack, anxiety that incapacitates, freezes, hyperventilating

A panic attack became a personal awakening for Dan Harris, the journalist, talk host, and the author of *10% Happier: How I Tamed the Voice in My Head, Reduced Stress Without Losing My Edge, and Found Self-Help That Actually Works.*

One of the most memorable – and painful to watch – anxiety attacks I've seen were Andrew Marr's, the show and interview on BBC. The show of the attack is where host struggles to get out words, coughs, gets some water to simply get the words out. Whilst the host admirably pulled through, the struggle is obvious and it's real. Coincidence or not, it is also the show where the host apologises for making the mistake from a show before. This might be an indication of additional pressure, adding to overwhelm. What is absolutely gobsmacking though, is that this anxiety attack might have been a prelude to the heart attack

Andrew Marr experienced couple of years later – the signs of panic attack can be an indication of the trouble ahead – just another example of how closely our bodies and minds are linked as well as the warning that if our body signals are ignored, it is often at our peril.

Andrew Marr is not the only host to suffer anxiety on live TV. Dan Harris, the author of '10% Happier', suffered 2 attacks live! This was his moment of awakening and a prelude to his great book, however, his attacks are shorter and don't feel as painful to watch as Andrew Marr's. But internally, all panic attacks are terrifying – I know that from personal experience.

Panic attacks tick the emotional overwhelm boxes. They are short, intense, and destructive. While both Dan Harris and Andrew Marr recovered fairly quickly (albeit painfully), recovery is not a given. I was once in an audience of 200 people when the presenter started stammering in the middle of his presentation. He never managed to finish it and had to be walked from the stage as he froze.

It can happen to anyone.

Here is what the **Emotional Footprint** for overwhelming fear could look like.

Step 1: R. - Recognize the signs early   47

Case Study - Fear

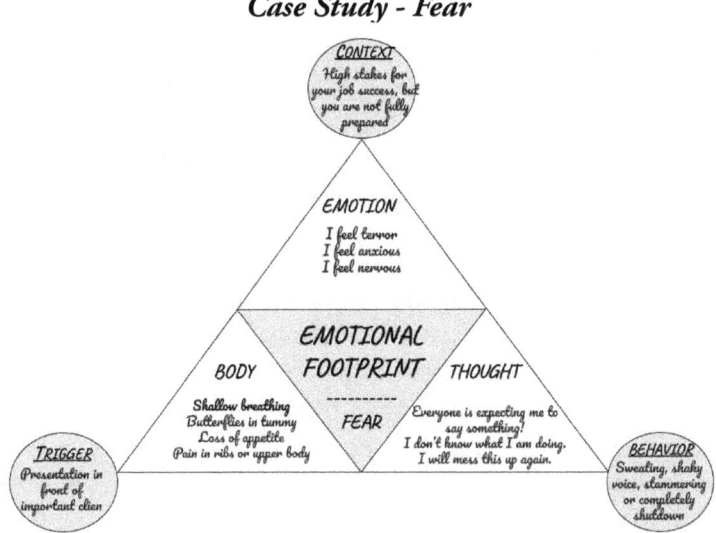

Figure 4 - Emotional Footprint of Fear

Ready to go deeper? As Seth Godin likes to emphasize, fear is the queen of emotions as it keeps us alive. This is why it is so powerful and can easily override everything else. Often, the overwhelming need could be as simple as getting to safety. Socially-triggered fear could be about an imagined or overblown interpretation of a threat, so thinking of ways to feel safe in those moments can help.

Overwhelming Embarrassment (Close to Shame and Even Disgust)

Potential body signals - red in the face, whole body shaking, literally running away from the situation

If there is one person that could be considered the embarrassment professional, it would be actress Jennifer Lawrence.

Everybody saw her lose half of her dress on the way to the Oscars, and that's not even the most embarrassing thing in her life. In her interview with Jimmy Fallon, she admits she once got star-struck with a woman she tough to be Elisabeth Taylor, who was dead at that time, and walking in a party with her dress unzipped the first time she was in Paris.

Embarrassment ticks all the emotional overwhelm boxes. It's short, it can be intense, and it feels destructive. It is also extremely social. We rarely feel embarrassed about spilling something alone. Jennifer Lawrence deals with it remarkably well. Her honesty and sense of humour disarm anyone who would use those moments against her. Overwhelming embarrassment can be truly destructive at work - you won't be able to put your ideas forward if you can't handle being embarrassed about saying something wrong or silly once in a while.

Case Study - Embarrassment

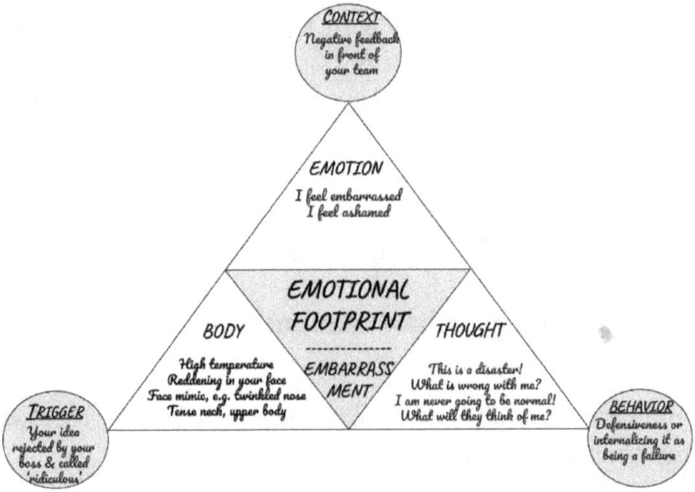

CONTEXT
Negative feedback in front of your team

EMOTION
I feel embarrassed
I feel ashamed

EMOTIONAL FOOTPRINT — EMBARRASSMENT

BODY
High temperature
Reddening in your face
Face mimic, e.g. twinkled nose
Tense neck, upper body

THOUGHT
This is a disaster!
What is wrong with me?
I am never going to be normal!
What will they think of me?

TRIGGER
Your idea rejected by your boss & called 'ridiculous'

BEHAVIOR
Defensiveness or internalizing it as being a failure

Figure 5 - Emotional Footprint of Embarrassment

Ready to go deeper? Shame and embarrassment often signal about an action outside of socially accepted norms, so your need could simply be to repair your social standing. It's important not to internalize the shameful event and to be practical about it. Nobody wants to lose half of their clothes at an important career event but embarrassing yourself doesn't define you. Jennifer Lawrence is not a loser despite embarrassing herself so often. She is an awesome human being, and so are you.

Overwhelming Sadness

Potential body signals - overwhelming need to cry, not wanting to do anything, feeling numb

I was in a group coaching session with Christian Mikkelsen, a famous coach, when he mentioned a dear friend of his who died recently. For a few minutes, Christian was so overwhelmed that he struggled to hold his tears back. His voice started quivering and he couldn't talk.

Some overwhelming situations offer flexibility. For example, Christian could have taken a break for a few minutes or rescheduled the session. Often, though, you can't do much except manage it. Sadness is generally a low-energy emotion, but it can be overwhelming. Notably, tears can be an expression of frustration (the cousin of anger) or helplessness (the cousin of sadness) or can invoke compassion and empathy.

Intense sadness ticks the boxes for hijacking. It's often short (the actual grieving process is long, but overwhelm goes quickly), intense, and quite destructive. It might hold us long enough to undermine our ability to continue with normal life.

Case Study - Sadness

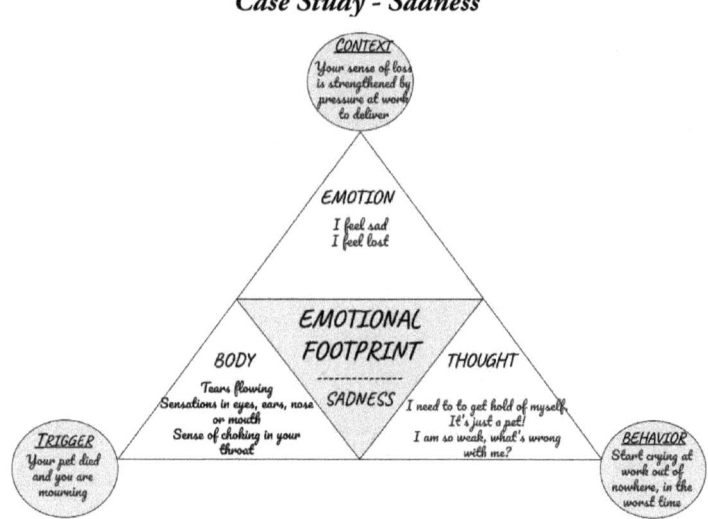

Figure 6 - Emotional Footprint of Sadness

Ready to go deeper? Sadness is a prosocial emotion. It tells others not to expect much from us for some time or that we need care[16]. Sadness numbs your pain from a loss, protecting you until you regain strength. Overwhelming tears of sadness could be signalling your need to retreat until you recover.

Overwhelming Shock (Related to Surprise)

Potential body signals - complete freezing or sense of numbing, being near-completely incapacitated

Being overwhelmed by shock is a short-lived and intense but not necessarily destructive experience. Most of us don't experience surprises every day. However, people can be so shocked they can't protect themselves. One time in a bar, I saw a man slap a woman. She was in such a shock, she completely froze. I took her out of the pub and arranged a cab home for her because she was not capable of making decisions.

Remember, emotional overwhelm often is about socially triggered threats rather than actual danger. A physical slap in the pub — no matter how despicable — was more about humiliation than a physical threat. The woman told me she had never been slapped before, let alone in front of many people.

Case Study - Shock

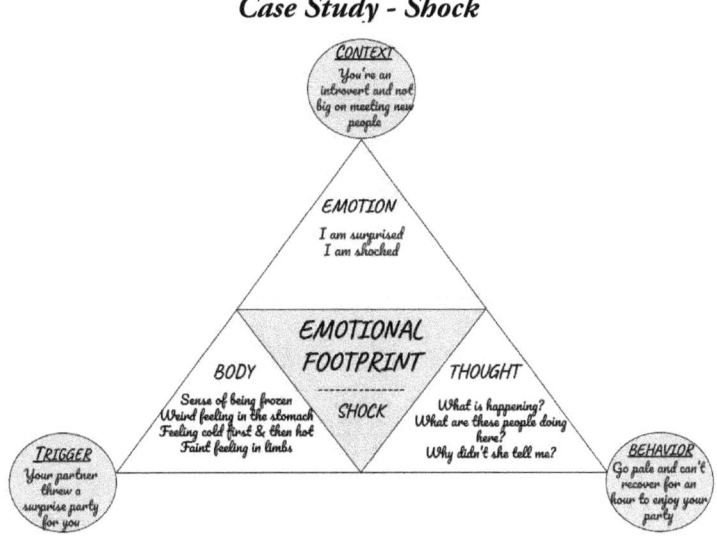

Figure 7 - Emotional Footprint of Shock

Ready to go deeper? The emotion of surprise gives us time to assess whether we need to protect ourselves from threats or move towards opportunities. From the emotion maps I referred to early in this chapter, it's clear that surprise is spread throughout the body, consistent with the need to assess the situation. So, managing your surprise in an overwhelming situation can help you get through your assessment quicker.

Overwhelming Joy

Potential body signals - inability to function appropriately, making poor decisions, or acting silly

When Gwyneth Paltrow receives her Oscar, she cries nonstop from the moment her name is announced, stammering through her speech. There is nothing wrong with crying when you are getting an Oscar or when you meet your idols, like kids who meet David Beckham or receive life-changing gifts from Ellen DeGeneres. However, it can be destructive. Overwhelming joy might prevent you from having a chat with your idol or even endanger you, e.g., walking into a street without checking for cars when you get excited. Overwhelming joy feels intense and is also quite short-lived, ticking the boxes of emotional overwhelm.

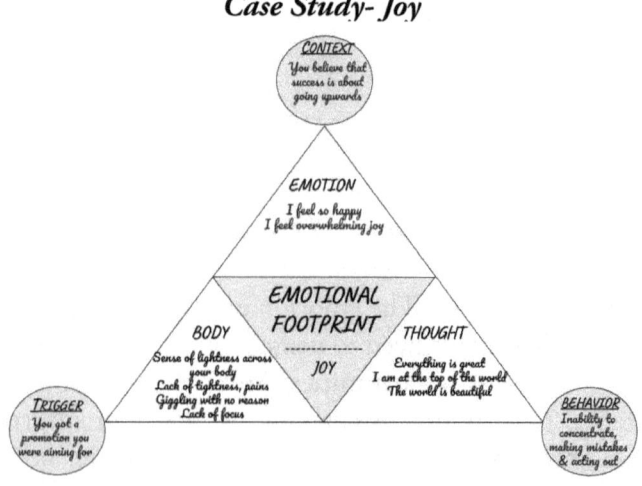

Figure 8 - Emotional Footprint of Joy

Step 1: R. - Recognize the signs early

Ready to go deeper? The need behind joy seems to be about pushing us towards events that bring it — essentially, to have more of the bliss. You feel good and then decide to have more of that in your life, although ideally, in a more controlled way so you wouldn't need to deal with overwhelm.

EXERCISE

Now that you know the key aspects of the six basic emotions, it's time to apply them in your life.

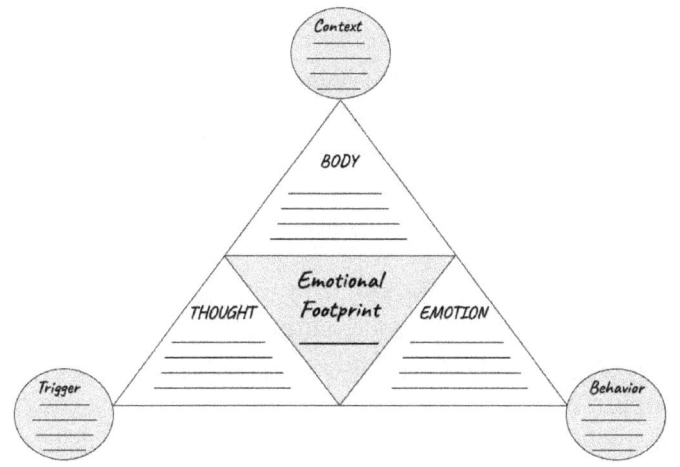

Figure 9 - Emotional Footprint BLANK

Think of one to three emotionally charged situations in which you behaved in ways you regretted later, for example:

1. You acted out your emotion and displayed it to others, like crying when you didn't want to.

2. You reacted internally in a way that hurt you, like freezing in front of an audience or not standing up to a bully.

Then, fill in the triangle tool below for each situation. You can download more sheets here.

Be aware. Emotions play an important role in memory retention, so you might re-experience your emotions intensely. While you want to be as specific as you can about your body and mind signals, you should prepare for potential discomfort or even pain. Make sure you do this exercise in an emotionally safe environment — either alone (to protect others or stop them from using your vulnerability) or with people who can be trusted. Also, plan something nice for yourself afterward to soothe yourself! ***Do NOT work on truly traumatic events without mental health professional guidance.***

Tip. Even if the signs you captured don't match helpful tools or diagrams, stay authentic to what you notice, think, and feel. While science hasn't settled the argument about how universal the expression of emotions is, you can sidestep it by simply recording what is relevant to you.

Mistake to avoid. Overthinking it. Stay with your thoughts too long, and you might start rationalizing your emotional hijacking or fall into victimhood. The key is to be observational without stewing on any aspect of your internal state. Remember, the goal is to get out of emotional overwhelm, not justify it. ------ ------

Step 1: R. - Recognize the signs early

In **Step 1**, you learned to recognize the signs of emotional overwhelm specific to you, to pick them up easily. You might even pick up some repetitive issues, e.g., notice that you get triggered by people with authority because of your low self-esteem. This knowledge might help you put up a safeguard to prevent emotional hijacking next time. In later chapters, I talk about prevention, but meanwhile, you need to give yourself more time.

Summary

1. To get out of emotional overwhelm, you need to recognize your body and mind's signs. The triangle tool helps capture those signs specific to you so that you can recognize them early and change the course of your behaviour.

2. The six case studies of emotional overwhelm are closely related to six basic emotions that are near-universal in humans.

3. The signs of emotional overwhelm are briefness, intensity, and destructive impact, internal or external.

STEP 2: I. - IMITATE A RELAXED BODY STATE

Expanding your body physiologically prepares you to be present; it overrides your instinct to fight or flee, allowing you to be grounded, open, and engaged.

– Amy Cuddy, *Presence: Bringing Your Boldest Self to Your Biggest Challenges*

There is a reason why Zidane lost it during the extra time and not in the first five minutes of the game. His tension was building all match. The last minutes of his career were ticking by. The stakes of the game were at an all-time high because France hadn't been in the World Cup final for more than a decade. The match had plenty of controversies — penalties, lost opportunities to score, disputable referee decisions. Extra time added to physical exhaustion, too. During the penalty shootout, many players were barely standing.

Even under such pressure, Zidane ignored Marco's provocation for a while, maybe focusing on the game and disregarding the noise. Only after a particular part of the mut-

Step 2: I. - Imitate A Relaxed Body State

tering (probably the more drastic insult) was he suddenly just over it.

This is how real life works. **The triggers that get us into emotional overwhelm are rarely isolated, short, or manageable incidents. More often than not, they feel like arrows coming at us from different directions, all at once.**

The advice to 'create a pause,' 'just breathe,' or 'step back' falls short because it fails to consider the complex reality of the socially triggered emotional behaviour. If you've ever been gripped by anger, you know that in its midst, 'stepping back' feels as possible as winning a million dollars. Even if you manage to 'count to 10' and calm down after an insult, the most minor thing can throw you off. For example, hearing someone laugh at the abuse might trigger you. Mental state matters as much as physical. Being stressed can make us less compassionate[17]. Remember how 'easy' it was to manage workplace conflict after a lousy night's sleep?

Our bodies are our first line of defence – They can register things (e.g., threats) much faster than we can formulate thoughts[18]. As such, our bodies are the best places to help stop emotional overwhelm. To maximize the chance of holding against such a powerful automated reaction, R.I.D.E doubles down on switching the body's response from high-intensity gear to a lower one. You achieve this by imitating the relaxed state through two science-backed techniques:

1. '2-t0-1 breath' technique that imitates relaxed breath
2. 'Relaxed posture', that mimics a relaxed body state By imitating a relaxed body, you switch from the highly

intense sympathetic nervous system response, responsible for gearing you to action and increased body's arousal, to parasympathetic, accountable for a relaxed and calm body state.

Both techniques have scientific evidence behind them. Notably, both techniques complement each other and can be done simultaneously, as outlined in the *Exercise* section below. While there are many physically-based ways to reduce emotional overwhelm — exercising is one of them — some are more helpful than others. If you're in a work meeting with a formidable client and an unsupportive boss, doing a few push-ups is not an option. Not all breathing techniques are equally suitable either — compare the short breaths to control pain of labour with the deep, relaxing breaths of meditation.

The positive power of breath has been researched extensively in the context of reducing high-stress responses and activation of parasympathetic nerve system[19]. While the process is not yet fully understood, it is increasingly evident that deep and slow breathing helps reduce the fight-or-flight response, often triggered by the amygdala. The '2-to-1 breath' technique is particularly suitable because it can be quickly deployed and works well in combination with relaxed posture. Research also shows that deep breathing might be one of the fastest ways to calm down as it directly connects to the brain's arousal center[20].

While the research into the power of posture is less conclusive, posture's impact on our mood has caused quite a stir in recent years. Amy Cuddy's research about the power pose and its influence on confidence has generated a lot of excitement, backlash, and further evidence. Her research proved that adopting a power posture helps people feel more powerful[21].

If you ever heard 'fake it until you make it,' you might not have realized there is science behind that, too. For example, in one study (that arguably is quoted one time too often), the participants who were forced to smile through pen-in-teeth exercises ended up reporting more positive emotions, potentially due to amygdala activation[22]. A recent study into the impact of open posture and defensive posture showed that a defensive position makes us feel worse while rearranging our posture to a more relaxed one, makes us feel better[23]. Upright posture can even relieve depressive symptoms[24]. While more research is required, it is clear that the mind and body are a two-way street in regard to moods and that changing our posture can dramatically shift how we feel.

2-to-1 Breath

It is a simple technique — you have twice as many exhalations as inhalations.

When you breathe in, count to three. When you breathe out, count to six. Do that a few times. Slowly increase your count when you are ready. For example, count to four for inhalation and to seven or eight for exhalation. It's not about precision - as long as your exhalation is significantly longer than your inhalation, you will achieve the same relaxed body imitation.

Relaxed posture

This technique is about imitating your most relaxed state without looking silly. A lie down in the middle of an argument is not advised!

Imagine yourself completely calm and peaceful — it doesn't matter whether it's your beach posture or meditation. What body signs mean a relaxed posture to you? Comfortable feeling in your head and neck? Loosened shoulders? Unlocked hands? The great thing about this technique is that the relaxed posture you want to imitate stays the same whether you are pulling yourself out of an angry outburst or an anxiety attack.

In the diagram below, look at an example of how the emotional footprint would look for calm.

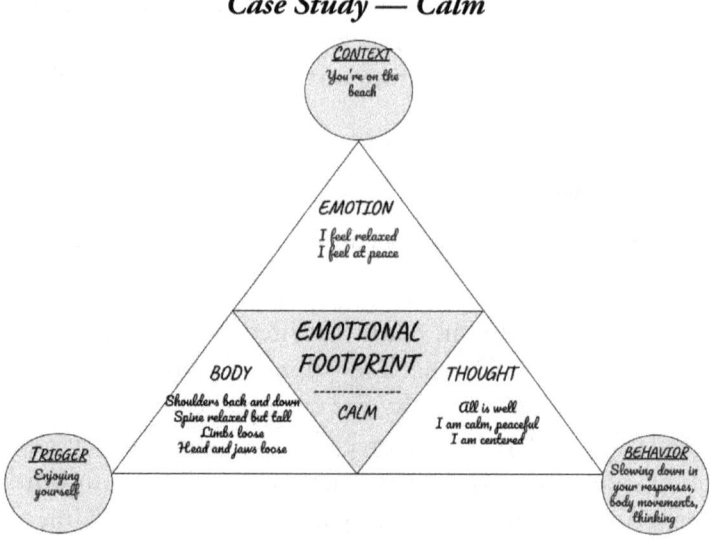

Figure 10 - Emotional Footprint of Calm

Combining these two techniques maximizes our chances of switching our body from a highly intense state to a more relaxed one, but they are not the only techniques that work. I added a couple of alternative relaxation strategies, should the '2-to-1 breath' and 'Relaxed posture' not suit you. R.I.D.E. doesn't need to be a rigid tool and can be amended according to everyone's needs and preferences, as long as the other techniques chosen are powerful enough and can be deployed subtly. The only thing to look out for in different strategies is that they often require prior skills. For example, visualization is complex unless you start with a teacher that can guide you well, and progressive muscle relaxation requires a few tries to pick up.

EXERCISE

> Think back to the situation you thought of in Step 1. When you feel the tension rising, you do the R — Recognize the signs in your body. For this exercise, let yourself feel those signs, even if it's unpleasant.
>
> Then do the following:
>
> 1. Fill in your emotional footprint for calm and relaxation. Use it for your imitation of the relaxed state. The more signs you can pick up, the easier it will be to switch your body from highly intense to a more relaxed state.

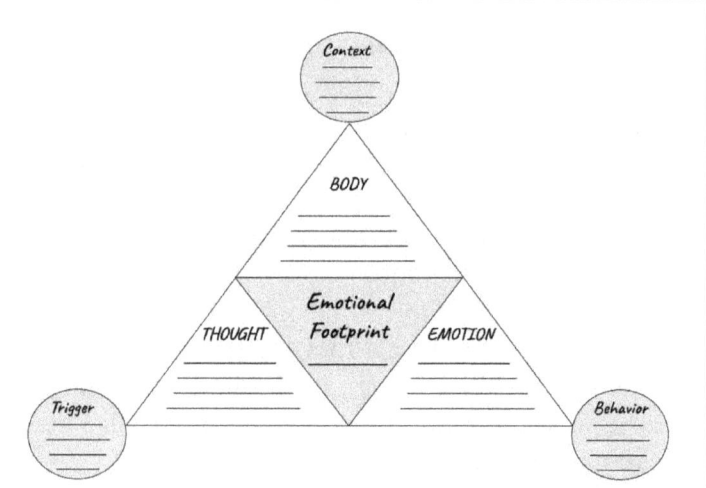

2. Inhale while counting to 2 and exhale counting to 4, making your first small change in your posture, like straightening your back. You should start feeling change immediately. If you are angry, this will get you a bit more straight instead of being in a hunched forward attack pose. If you are anxious, this will get you a bit more stable instead of scattered. If you were just about to cry and felt helpless, it will change your posture into a more straight and strong posture instead of a pose of retreat.

3. Inhale to 3 and exhale to 6. Purposefully lower and relax your shoulders and upper back (or follow your signs from your emotional footprint).

4. Inhale to 4 and exhale to 8, relaxing your hands, including palms and wrists. You can even shake them a little bit.

5. Repeat until you feel more in control, following your signs one by one. You might put your legs fully on the ground so that your whole body can be supported entirely.

Whatever you do, keep your exhalations twice as long as your inhalations to maximize the impact. Ideally, make one different posture change with each cycle of breath.

Be aware. Your breathing shouldn't be too loud or too visible as it defeats the purpose of controlling your emotional overwhelm properly. If you are hyperventilating, breathing out so loud that everybody can hear or holding your breath until passing out, keep practising until you don't.

PRO TIP. Don't be afraid to take your time to breathe and calm down. While we do often need to respond quickly in highly intense situations, giving yourself and the opponent, a few moments is one of the best things to do in an argument. By letting others talk, you make them feel heard and respected. It also gives them more time to manage their stress and overwhelm, instead of feeling attacked by your clever arguments. Listening solves more problems than arguments, so taking time to do your deep breathing and posture changes is not as bad as it sounds.

Mistake to avoid. Stop breathing. While some heated moments will quickly pass with just deep breathing or imagining feeling grounded, it rarely is enough to fully get you out of emotional overwhelm. Just because your body switched gears, doesn't mean you are out of the woods completely, so you need the next R.I.D.E. steps to master.

Alternative strategies:

1. **Visualization.** Visualization is powerful. It's not me saying that but science. For example, studies have shown that we can learn things just by watching them[25]. We can also achieve great results only by visualizing them. So, to manage emotional overwhelm, imagining your happy place might get you there. The trick is to practice it first to be able to get to that place even in the midst of emotional overwhelm, which is almost a whole new habit in itself.

Exercise.

1. Visualize your happy place where you feel safe, relaxed, and content. Ideally, you recognize it easily to access it quickly. Imagine being there with as much detail as you can - the smells, the feeling, the sounds, the earth beneath your feet. The more real it feels, the more easily you can imitate that state realistically.

2. If you struggle to find your happy place, try a tree grounding visualization. This aligns well with the '2-to-1 breath' technique.
   - *With your first exhalation*, position your feet fully on the ground, a bit apart, to properly support your whole body.

- *With your second exhalation*, imagine your feet as the roots of a strong, big tree, reaching deep into the Earth.
- *With your third exhalation*, imagine the water and energy going up the root to the trunk, bringing nutrients to you.
- *With your fourth exhalation*, feel how grounded to the earth you are now that your feet are so entrenched in Earth.
- *With your fifth exhalation*, imagine how strong you are, with your arms being branches of the tree and your upper body being the whole crown of the tree. This keeps you stable, strong, powerful, and calm.

2. **Progressive muscle relaxation.** This technique is based on science, too.[26] If you tense your muscles long enough, they will HAVE to relax. It's a powerful technique to FORCE your body into relaxation. The tricky part is doing this with the group of muscles that is the tensest to achieve the greatest impact as it takes about eight to ten seconds to work. To use it during emotional overwhelm, you only have one shot and can target one group of muscles, but it's a powerful technique when done right.

Exercise.

1. To maximise the impact, try progressive muscle relaxation with '2-to-1 breath'. After inhalation, hold your breath and while you do that, target the

> tensest muscle group. If you don't know where to start for the maximum impact, try with your upper body. Make your neck, shoulders, and jaw as tense as you can for the eight to ten seconds. If you have more time, do it with another group of muscles. For example, if you are clenching your fist, just clench it for eight to ten seconds as much as you can, up until it hurts. Once you let go, the muscle must relax; it has no choice in the matter. Because relaxed muscles require less oxygen, this technique will also feed your slower breath cycle[27]. However, it can take time to learn to apply subtly in tense situations.

In this chapter, you learned how to gain a few seconds during emotional overwhelm to calm down. Those seconds are precious because they give you a chance to change the course of your behaviour and insert better, more appropriate, and powerful responses. However, many intense situations are multi-layered and complex, with multiple triggers and complex social context so relying only on the body is not enough to fully calm down. In the next chapter, you will learn how to bring the power of emotions to help you, not hinder you, by inviting compassion into the picture.

Summary

1. I. is about *imitating a relaxed state* to reduce emotional overwhelm in your body and give you time to insert appropriate responses.
2. Using your *body and posture* at the same time maxi-

mizes your chances of reducing your physiological response to emotional overwhelm, giving you more time.

3. Alternative strategies, like visualization or muscle relaxation, can be powerful but require more practice and preparation to work.

STEP 3: D - DEPLOY SELF-COMPASSION

Emotions are one of the most powerful tools we have.

- David Desteno, Emotional Success

One person from the IT team was so demanding, inconsiderate, or just plain rude that he often triggered my own most hot-headed behaviours. Instead of searching for the cause of the problem, he demanded 'to fix it immediately.' Instead of contributing to a solution, he criticized others' ideas or looked for scape goats. Worst of all, he never changed. You could count on him being this way any time, never learning from before, always expecting everyone else to change instead.

You might have someone like that in your life, too — often at the center of the argument, strong enough to stand their ground until everyone else gives up. In the best-case scenario, such a toxic person is a peer or an acquaintance. In the worst case, it's someone in your family or your boss.

If there is someone like this in your family, you know how unpleasant and exhausting Christmas break can be. All weekend, you are trying to control yourself, but even if you hold on for a while, you eventually snap, as bottled-up emotions can only be pushed away until the stress becomes too great[28].

The common wisdom suggests cognitive strategies to manage such toxic people. You are expected to stay calm and centered no matter what it takes — suppressing your anger ('count to 10'), being rational ('this will not matter in five years') or taking a step back ('it's probably not personal'). The more advanced strategies suggest remembering your values and long-term goals ('I am much better off not over-reacting here') or thinking of three reasons why this person could be acting this way ('he is probably stressed at home').

For people who we don't need to deal with every day, this might work, but even then, it can be exhausting because it adds to our cognitive load and depletes us[29]. Needing to manage someone toxic everyday can break us.

To manage intense situations when we are already depleted, more potent tools are needed, and we would struggle to find something more powerful than emotions at our disposal. Step 3 is about purposefully engaging our emotions to purposefully changing our emotional state to something better.

David DeSteno, the author of *Emotional Success: The Power of Gratitude, Compassion, and Pride*, notes that from a motivational perspective, emotions are much more powerful than relying on willpower, reason, or executive function. He names gratitude, compassion, and pride as the three most powerful positive emotions[30]. All of those emotions can work in emotional overwhelm too. For example, when

I was overwhelmed by sadness at my friend's death, it helped me to feel *grateful* for having known him. When I felt furious at my ex for pushing me around, I did manage to pull myself together by deploying *pride* – 'I am better than this'.

However, despite being powerful, *gratitude* and *pride* can be hard to apply at a moment's notice. For example, trying to feel grateful about a bully who is harassing you is saint material. Even *pride* and *compassion* require practice to cultivate on purpose so that they can pull you out of an emotional situation without undermining your emotional safety.

Self-compassion is a much more comfortable place to start. It is as powerful as *compassion*, but much easier to apply in an overwhelming moment.

Self-Compassionate Perspective Technique

Self-compassion offers something that no other emotion does — the ability to feel negative emotions but not be lost in them. It validates our pain without having that pain define us and it unlocks connection with others rather than increasing separation that leads to more pain.

The trick is to deploy *self-compassion* quickly enough to help in an intense situation. Ideally, we would practice *self-compassion* as a habit to forgive ourselves for our mistakes and failures every day. We don't have a lot of time during emotional overwhelm, so instead, we quickly deploy three core elements of *self-compassion*, as defined by the most known *self-compassion* researcher, Dr. Kristine Neff:

1. Mindfulness
2. Kindness towards self
3. Finding common humanity.

Luckily, **Triangle Tool** is all about mindfulness, so we only need to deploy the other two — kindness and common humanity – in addition to what we have already learned about mindfulness.

Validation of our pain is at the core of kindness towards self. Once we validate our right to feel the negative intense emotion, we stop needing external acknowledgement. **We stop needing someone else's approval because we give it to ourselves.** To strengthen the power of this technique, we will combine it with the 'third-person' technique that has been shown to help reduce emotional reactivity without increasing mental load.

EXERCISE

> Think back to one situation in which you really lost your control and regretted it.
>
> Run quickly through the first two steps, recognizing the signs and imitating the relaxed state brings mindfulness in the picture.

Now you should add three more things:

1. **Name what you feel.** For example, it may be 'I feel really sad about my friend dying last week' (labelling emotion to reduce emotional intensity)

2. **Treat yourself with kindness, validate your pain.** 'Lina, you are feeling sad. You are grieving.' ('Third-person' technique to give space)

3. **Bring common humanity.** 'Lina, you feel sad and it's okay. Everyone loses someone they love. Everyone grieves.' (The beginning of connection)

If you feel ashamed, here is how it could look:

1. I am so embarrassed!

2. Lina, you made a fool out of yourself today, but it's okay to feel ashamed for a moment.

3. Lina, everybody makes mistakes. Everybody is ashamed about something. It's okay.

If you feel anger, here is how it could look:

1. This is so unfair! I am so angry!

2. Lina, it's okay to feel frustrated. Anyone would when their needs are undermined.

3. Lina, everybody feels angry sometimes. It's normal. It's human.

PRO TIP. Keep the naming and validation of emotions short. The last thing you want to do is get stuck in emotion — positive or negative. Judging, ruminating, sulking, and wallowing keeps you there for much longer, but positive emotions can also backfire and evolve into mania-like behaviours.

Be aware. Self-compassion is a nuanced emotion, and it's easy, instead of validating your emotion, to justify your actions ('Anyone would be angry if they were treated this way!') or use it as an excuse not to change your behaviour. Keep yourself honest and resist the temptation to establish who is right.

Mistake to avoid. Feeling sorry for yourself. Self-compassion is NOT about making excuses, justifying your actions, or wallowing in your pain. It's not always a clear line to walk, but with practice, it becomes easier to separate your ability to be kind to yourself from playing a victim or justifying lack of action.

Alternative strategy. The idea behind the Emotional Scale, proposed by Abraham-Hicks, is simple — different emotions have different intensity (think rage/anger/frustration levels), so we can slowly climb from the most negative ones to fewer negative ones, thus reducing emotional intensity. For example, if you find yourself at the 'lowest' end of the scale, you will be experiencing highly negative emotions, such as hate or rage. To reduce that intensity, you can go slowly up that scale by feeling anger or revenge instead. When you stay with that emotion a bit, you can go higher

> up. It is a widely used technique and can be helpful. However, it is arguable whether feeling revenge is that much better than feeling rage. It might also be hard to have enough time to climb to a reasonable emotion during the emotional hijacking.

As you can guess, my problems with the aforementioned IT guy didn't go away. People rarely change to the extent we want them to. However, switching my emotion from anger and frustration to a more compassionate approach, I was more capable of handling him. The first time, I had a contentious encounter with heated arguments and not-so-nice words exchanged. The second time, I managed to act professionally through emails while still venting my frustration off to another person. He didn't mind, so nobody was hurt. The third time, I just sighed a bit and — still ensuring he doesn't cross my boundaries — managed to not get upset at all.

It works!

Summary

1. D. is about deploying self-compassion as a positive force to counter an overwhelmingly negative one, and doing it with mindfulness, kindness, and searching for common humanity.
2. Feeling more during the emotional overwhelm sounds counterintuitive, but it works quicker than suppression, reasoning, or other cognitive approaches that exhaust us.

Step 3: D - Deploy Self-Compassion 75

3. By using a 'third-person' technique, we can increase distance from the situation without overloading ourselves mentally.

STEP 4: E – EVOKE CONNECTION

Find a link - any link - to others.

- David Desteno, Emotional Success

One of the ideas Stephen Covey introduces in *The 7 Habits of Highly Effective People* is a 'paradigm shift' — an instant, powerful change in your perspective of a situation.

In the book, the author shares a mini paradigm shift he experienced on the way to work. As he and other passengers in a subway car were quietly reading newspapers, a couple of kids started harassing them. Stephen Covey was irritated enough to ask their father to intervene. The father said, 'Oh, you're right. I guess I should do something about it. We just came from a hospital where their mother died about an hour ago. I don't know what to think, and I guess they don't know how to handle it either.' In a split second, Mr. Covey saw his whole paradigm shift as he became more understanding, accepting, and keen to help.

While the author then discusses how to evoke such a shift in character through core principles and values, his story illustrates much more the power of emotions than values. Logically, the author was not better off knowing the fact the children just lost their mother — they were still disruptive, and their father was still absent in action. Understanding the reasons or even tapping into the values rarely changes the situation. It only adds a mental load on the psyche on top of everything else — irritation, the stress of getting to work, and thinking of what to do. For the values to be strong enough to help in emotionally overwhelming situations, they need to be lived and practised every day. Unfortunately, we don't revisit them often enough for it to happen. The last time I reviewed mine, I named creativity, fun, and challenge as core until the trainer reminded us to name values based on past decisions. It turned out that the values I actually lived by were safety, integrity, and connection — not even close to my initial guesses. Unless our heads and hearts align — a rare occurrence in a stressful situation — we will have difficulty choosing our values over our desires and impulses when under stress.

No, what moved Stephen Covey towards such powerful and swift acceptance was his empathy for the family's pain. What touched him so much that he even suggested help was not his logic or values but his compassion.

Bringing compassion into an emotionally overwhelming situation is one of the most powerful things you can do. It can instantly turn around how you feel about a problem, reducing the intense negative feeling of anger, sadness, or shame.

Compassion is an inherently social emotion. Nine out of ten times, our need to control our emotional overwhelm includes other people. Compassion's social nature means that we subconsciously invite social, rather than individual, benefits in the situation. We switch gears from working towards the same direction rather than 'us versus me' or 'he is a jerk, and I am right' type of thinking.

Compassion also has shown to resist one psychological phenomenon that other tools struggle with — temporal discounting. It is a human tendency to decrease the value of things in the future in favour of things now. While it sounds technical, we do this daily. We value beautiful bodies of the future less than the pleasure of food now, the joy of shopping today over the value of the money saved later, and so on. It isn't such a stretch to see the parallel of valuing the unleashing of our anger, releasing our tears, and jumping out of the room to relieve emotional tension immediately instead of staying calm to achieve our long-term goals. In fact, immediate relief can be so tempting that it can wipe out any residual willpower, logical arguments, and values. Compassion helps manage that pressing gratification by feeling compassion towards our own future-self, making it easier to save, eat, or act well.

The only tricky thing is bringing compassion into the emotionally overwhelming situation quickly and subtly. Luckily, there is one effortless way to do that — to **evoke connection**, any connection, with the other.

Evoking Connection Technique

No matter how scary or nasty the client yelling at you is, he is still a son, a brother, or a father to someone. No matter how angry you are at someone who just insulted you, you are similar in more ways than you imagine — even if it's just fondness of the same cafe. No matter how overwhelm-

Step 4: E – Evoke Connection

ing sadness can be, knowing that people around you felt the same at some point in their lives, unites us as humans.

Sharing anything can connect people, but sharing pain helps us see each other less as 'the enemy' or 'the opponent' and instead a fellow human. Instead of 'us versus them,' it becomes 'we,' no matter how different the corners you find yourselves in any particular situation.

EXERCISE

> Think back to a situation in which you really lost your control and didn't want to.
>
> Run quickly through the R.I.D. steps - **Recognize** your signs, **Imitate a relaxed state** and **deploy compassion** towards yourself.
>
> Once you go through these three steps, to **evoke connection**, you only need to remember one thing that might connect to the person who you felt angry with, cried in front of, or felt embarrassed in front of.
>
> **PRO TIP**. In a rare case of feeling overwhelmed while alone, for example, hyperventilating before the flight, you can evoke a connection with someone from your life — a friend or family member. Reminding yourself that everybody feels scared, sad, or overwhelmed helps further build on the common humanity that brings self-compassion while connecting with people. Even panic attacks — often, a solitary affair — can be managed by remembering you are not alone in your struggles.

Be aware. This step is not appropriate in every situation! If you are being abused or even under threat, it is NOT the time to bring compassion for a person and say, 'poor thing.' When someone is attacking you verbally, emotionally, or physically, you need a safe exit strategy and then you need to think about preventing this next time.

Mistake to avoid. It might be tempting to seek something substantial for your connection. We consciously and unconsciously seek out connections with people around us. Finding a robust connection like knowing that your boss is concerned about team results to is also likely to evoke more powerful results. Unfortunately, we rarely find ourselves in emotionally charged situations with people we already have strong connections with. It is often with our polar-opposites, and in polar-opposite situations, that we get overwhelmed. Instead, it is smarter to focus on easy things such as liking the same colour, or both being Beatles fans. Sometimes just remembering that we are both humans seeking success is enough.

Alternative strategy. If you feel like compassion is too hard to invite into emotional overwhelm, try *pride*. *Pride* is an underrated emotion because it brings conflicting feelings, but it can help with strengthening motivation. Instead of relying on connection with the person, which might be problematic in a hostile environment, remember that you can do better than that. You can try to tap into your *pride* of being a 'better you' - someone who manages to stay calm under pres-

> sure and who takes pride in their ability to stay focused on goals and life values.

In this chapter, you learned to finish off your emotional hijacking by inviting strong positive emotions to transform the strong negative ones. Now you can practice R.I.D.E. from start to finish and even try it out in real-life situations.

Just as our emotions and reactions are not linear, the success of mastering your self-control is not linear either. Two steps forward and one step back is a good rule of thumb to adopt when progressing forward. It's important to not set yourself up for failure by seeing every mistake or mishap as a lack of progress. In the next chapter, you will see how marginal success can still be worth celebrating.

Summary

1. E. is about **evoking connection** with people in an intense situation to bring in a strong positive emotion, *compassion*, to replace a strong negative one.

2. Self-control usually includes other people, therefore social emotions do a great job of switching the perspective from 'me' to 'we.'

3. Compassion also helps us manage the need for immediate gratification, like venting, that makes self-control possible and even easy.

SECTION III -
SET YOURSELF UP FOR SUCCESS TO GET OUT OF EMOTIONAL HIJACKING

R.I.D.E. IN PRACTISE

Sweat more in practise, bleed less in war.

— Spartan Warrior Credo

All human interactions can become emotionally charged in seconds, even with people you like and respect. As a Highly Sensitive Person, I deal with emotional overwhelm daily. A rude person can set off my anger in seconds. A critical remark can undermine my productivity or motivation for days, and it can take me years to recover from failure or embarrassment.

While describing the process of R.I.D.E. takes a while, applying it only takes seconds to make a difference between emotionally driven behaviour and the ability to leave an intense situation on your own terms.

Recently, I was providing a recommendation about one of my projects to the team. My boss disagreed with the proposed steps, and he questioned the research behind it in front of the team! Signs of emotions only took milliseconds to note:

- **Step 1** — Cheeks getting red, temperature rising, my upper body tensing.
- **Step 2** – Immediately, I started relaxing my posture with deep breathing, purposefully pulling back my shoulders, opening my neck, loosening my jaw, and unclenching my hands (Relaxing takes a few seconds, but my opponent — in this case, my boss — was talking. As mentioned before, taking the time to relax had a side benefit of making me look more attentive. While it's not proper deep listening, it's still a much better alternative to using that time trying to suppress your emotional reaction.)
- **Step 3** – Once my boss finished talking, I was still tense and my voice was still strained, as I still felt annoyed. So, I told myself, 'Lina, it's true this sounds unfair. Everybody would feel angered by the implied assumption you didn't do your job. That's okay. You know what you did. Everybody feels angry sometimes.' (*Self-compassion* is easy to apply in the moment and reduces emotional intensity immediately. It's like going from boiling water to the warm temperature you enjoy in the bath, as long as you don't allow yourself to get stuck on the unfairness or justification of your actions. And yet, the emotional overwhelm was not over. I still had to deal with the situation on my terms. My effort was questioned, in front of people whose respect I needed, so the emotions were still strong and could flare up at any time. In other words, I needed something even stronger!).

- **Step 4** - So, I did the **E. - Evoked Connection** with my boss in the hope of bringing compassion into the mix. It wasn't hard. While we are different people, I know that he is a kind and fair person who was keen to ensure the task was done right. Knowing that we want the same thing, albeit not necessarily through the same solutions, was enough for me to calm down. (Fully, this time!)

The situation wasn't ideal. My anger was obvious to everyone. And yet, the situation de-escalated without a significant dispute. We successfully came to a solution that suited both sides and did so professionally while saving face in front of the team.

It can be that simple.

Of course, this was a small incident even in my life. Still, happiness and success are often more defined by small incidents than by big ones. We often place great importance on the big things in our lives — the first job, the first love, the big failures or big successes — but it is the quality of our first coffee of the day or a nice chat with a colleague that often makes our days better and brighter.

Getting your daily emotional overwhelms under control leads to better decisions, which lead to better relationships, which lead to a better life — receiving promotions, being happier at work, and forging stronger social connections.

R.I.D.E. is not a 100% guarantee. Nothing in life is. However, having it at your disposal means you will have more tools to use when you need them; you'll be more prepared and in control even before you enter an emotionally overwhelming situation. All you need to do is practice and make it your own.

In the rest of the chapters, you will learn how to not set yourself up for failure when you start.

Summary

1. R.I.D.E. is a tool that can get you out of emotional hijacking or highly emotional situations in seconds.
2. The tool can be applied in various situations, with most intense emotions, without putting too much strain on your cognitive load.
3. The power of R.I.D.E. is not just in simplicity, but in the practise.

WHAT SUCCESSFUL EMOTIONAL CONTROL LOOKS LIKE

'Anybody can become angry. That is easy, but to be angry with the right person, and to the right degree, and at the right time, and for the right purpose, and in the right way is not within everybody's power. That is not easy.'

Aristotle

After his panic attack on live television, Dan Harris went on a quest to tame his own demons. During this journey to understand the path to happiness and enlightenment, he interviewed many contemporary spiritual leaders and self-help gurus – including Eckhart Tolle, Deepak Chopra, and His Holiness Dalai Lama. In one of his conversations, Dan Harris asked His Holiness, 'Is your mind always calm?' Dalai Lama responded, 'No, no, no. Occasionally lose my temper[31].', then proceeding to joke that if someone never lose theirs, maybe they come from another space.

If His Holiness Dalai Lama can get angry, so can you. It doesn't make you a monster or weak. It makes you human.

Now that we know that there is no such thing as 100% success, we can move on to see what to aim for with our emotions.

Many assume that the goal of emotional mastery is to suppress our emotional expressions — stop our angry outbursts or fountains of tears. It is partly true – we do want to prevent the most destructive part of emotional overwhelm, our emotionally driven behaviours. But it's only a partial goal, not the end goal. For hours after an emotionally overwhelming incident, we can hold stress hormones silently but destructively, impacting our mental and physical health. Did you ever admire how calm sports referees look when players, fans, and even coaches yell at them? Their ability to control their emotions in the face of pure abuse might look remarkable, but the truth is much darker. Many referees have short careers, experience burnout, and have other mental health issues due to the physical and psychological toll from receiving personal attacks and even death threats.

Another mistake is to try to care less. Just like some doctors who perhaps have seen one death too many, we may opt out of our emotions to reduce their impact on us. However, becoming indifferent is not the answer. Emotions are a natural and often helpful signal about our internal state. Suppressing those signals can backfire because we ignore something important to us. If we suppress our emotions, we suppress positive ones too, often becoming numb and empty as a result.

We can only manage our emotions healthily and sustainably when we accept emotions as a valuable and vital part of us and seek the balance between what we feel and what we choose to show.

Since such a big part of this journey is internal, it is hard to capture truly successful emotional mastery examples. People we often assume are masters, can be suffering internally, and those who show emotion and restraint can be inauthentic. Emotional overwhelm happens to pretty much everyone so there are ways to see external signs of success and failures, which I outline below.

Emotional Mastery - LEVEL 1

The one thing that signals progress in managing controlling your emotional overwhelm is when you stop your behaviour, even if your emotional expression is visible. Showing anger but not headbutting the opponent, aggressive hand gestures but not punches in Ukrainian parliament, or being overcome by fear but not hyperventilating. Those are examples of the first level of mastery.

If you are triggered, feeling and looking emotional - but are not acting it out – congratulations, you have achieved Level 1!

Case study - Tony Abbott, a video called 'Speechless.' Tony Abbott, the former Prime Minister of Australia, had more than a few awkward moments during his tenure. Eating a raw onion without a blink or being the recipient of then PM Julia Gillard's 'Misogyny speech' – voted the most unforgettable T.V. moment in Australia[32] - are just a few examples. In the video 'Speechless,' he is aggressively pursued by a journalist to answer a question. He looks awkward and uncomfortable when he stammers out that they took his words out of context. Frankly, he looks weird. And yet, did you notice him hitting or headbutting the reporter? Does he yell or push him? Does he personally attack him or verbally abuse him? No! And that is progress. He even manages to squeeze out a response, 'You get the answer you deserve.' While snarky and not believable, he is on his way to controlling himself fully.

Ideal? No.

Progress? Yes!

Here are a few signs of Level 1 of Emotional Mastery:
- You care less and less about the traffic on the way to work or somebody cutting in front of you on the road.
- You leave a meeting and feel less stressed, annoyed, or frustrated than usual.
- You feel more in control even when the situation is stressful because you know you have tools at your disposal any time.
- When angry, you vent to someone else instead of to the person you are angry at, potentially saving a relationship.
- You feel on the verge of tears less often.

Emotional Mastery - LEVEL 2

The most important sign of progress at level 2 is the adequacy of your reaction.

Case study: Princess Diana's speech asking the media for 'time and space.' Princess Diana was arguably the most stalked person of all time. Her life started as a fairy-tale - married a prince, captivated hearts with her beauty, personality, and style - and made her the object of admiration and envy. But with the love triangle, the painful divorce, and having the beautiful princes as sons, her status as the Number One target of paparazzi was unavoidable till the end of her life -and even after. While initially, she had an amicable relationship with the media, such attention took an increasingly significant toll on her life. One day, she asked them to give her some time and space. In the video, you see how admirable her speech is, how courteous she is, and how nicely she is asking. Despite that, you can see she is nervous. It was visible to guests interviewed after the speech. In one of the documentaries, interviewees commented on how nervous and shaky she looked before the speech. By then, she has had years of experience dealing with the press!

Princess Diana did well in managing her emotions. She was collected and, while not calm, at least didn't display the signs of a shaky voice, starting to cry, or awkward silences.

This speech is an excellent example of emotional mastery, showing emotion, but adequately — not too much, not too little, and certainly not allowing emotions to overwhelm you!

Here are a few other clues for this stage of Level 2 Emotional Mastery:

- You notice that your emotional overwhelm incidents are increasingly rarer – occurring maybe once a week, or even once a month, or less.

- Eventually, emotional overwhelm incidents only happen when serious events happen or multiple triggers occur at once.
- Instead of shouting at someone, you are only irritated and use a cranky voice.
- Despite your best efforts, you can't fully control your emotional expression, but you leave the situation without significant hiccups. Perhaps people can see you got emotional, but you manage to come up with the solution and agree on a course of action.

Emotional Mastery - LEVEL 3

Case Study: Obama's tears during his gun violence speech. The Sandy Hook Primary School shooting that targets little kids is not something that most of us can brush off. The Sandy Hook shooting was one of the events that shook many inside and outside of America. President Obama sheds tears during the speech about gun violence and its impact but continues in an unwavering speech that there is work to be done to prevent this. Political views aside, the President needs to be able to continue no matter how overwhelmed he (or she) is.

True mastery is a balance between what you feel, what you express, and how you express it to ensure the best outcome in emotionally overwhelming situations. Aristotle's quote from thousands years ago still reflects true mastery the best — to feel your feelings, to be able to show them, but also to not let yourself be overwhelmed by them to the point where you cannot continue doing your job.

The signs of Level 3 Emotional Mastery are as follows:
- You allow yourself to feel your emotions, sometimes very strongly, but don't feel the need to express them in destructive ways.
- You direct the strength of your feelings with purpose towards more positive emotions.
- You can evoke compassion to yourself and others at a moment's notice, even in hostile situations.

Other Levels of Progress

Other levels of progress are worth knowing: the 'pre,' the 'post,' and the 'between.'

1. When you notice the signs but still lash out or cry, it's progress because your awareness is enhanced, enabling the first steps of change (pre-level).

2. When you notice the signs, get overwhelmed anyway, but then forgive yourself despite doing so (post-level), showing self-compassion towards your failures will help you later with your achievements.

3. If you do well one day, but not the next (between). Eric Greitens, in his book Resilience, notes that Greek philosophers knew that you could perform well one day and poorly the next. One bad day doesn't undermine your achievements, so it's important to keep going.

Here are a few other clues on this stage:
- You have more energy because you worry less.
- You get less irritated and frustrated about trivial things.

- When you worry or get upset, it's about more meaningful and important things.
- You feel more connected to other people and see them as fellows who also feel and suffer, not the jerks out to get you.
- Incredibly, you start feeling more sometimes. Because you freed up so much energy from your daily frustrations, you start noticing the beautiful things around you — even if it's just a blooming bush or a genuine and warm smile of the colleague. Those things you took for granted, never noticing them or appreciating them, are suddenly part of your day.

Now it's just about keeping up the work.

In this chapter, you saw some examples of successful emotional mastery and now know what to aim for. In the next chapter, you will learn to **R.I.D.E.** a habit to make your more intelligent and more compassionate responses actually become your automatic responses.

Summary

1. While neither R.I.D.E. nor any other tool guarantees 100% success, celebrating the signs of success, no matter how small, will keep you going.
2. The ultimate mastery of emotional overwhelm is not successful suppression or feeling less; it's the ability to handle your emotions but show them appropriately.

3. Even the most minor signs of success, like recognizing the signs in your body, will help you unlock the other levels.

HOW TO MAKE R.I.D.E. A HABIT

You do not rise to the level of your goals. You fall to the level of your systems.

- James Clear, Atomic Habits.

With R.I.D.E., you have a tool that can get you back into the driving seat during emotionally charged situations. However, if it isn't integrated into your day, R.I.D.E. will stay something to remember. When you do remember, you will use it and feel more in control, less exhausted, and less riled up afterward, but only until the stress becomes too high and you forget it, or until you're exhausted, hungry, or sleepless and have zero interest in managing the rising conflict, giving your emotions free reign.

For R.I.D.E. to help you effortlessly when you are caught up in a heat of the moment, it needs to become a habit.

A study at the University of California demonstrated that both good and bad habits persisted when people were stressed, not as a result of willpower or motivation[33].

Fighting millions of years of evolution that sculpted our bodies and tailored our minds into the most sophisticated tools on earth won't be easy, but just like millions of people managed to change their habits based on sugar or fat cravings despite being biologically programmed to want them, we are able to change our emotional responses to healthier ones.

While new research on habits is coming out every day, the principles behind habit-making stay remarkably similar. Since our automatic responses in emotionally overwhelming situations are like habits, it's worth delving deeper into habit science to make them work for us, not against us.

One of the critical things to remember is that the habits are repetitive. In other words, they often happen in loops. James Clear separates the habit loop's four core elements: **cue, craving, response, and reward**.

The answers that fuel the habit are captured in the Body-Emotion-Thought Triangle. This is where the **craving** (strong need to respond to social threat) that powers the habit lies. Your emotions and thoughts lead to interpretation and a **response** (emotionally driven behaviour) — unleashing your anger, letting go of your tears, or showing your embarrassment. The triangle also holds the key for the **reward** — the relief that comes with satisfying the need. It can be challenging to accept, but the short-term rewards can be powerful, such as the satisfaction of unleashing your anger or incredible relief that comes with tears. Even our fear-based reactions like hyperventilating work to relieve the pressure and jumping out of the room when embarrassed brings a sense of physiological and psychological safety.

Of course, those cravings and rewards that we get from releasing our emotions during emotional overwhelm often do not serve our long-term goals or fit social norms. To change, we reshape those critical aspects of the habit loop to form a new habit.

In *Atomic Habits*, James Clear talks about the four laws of changing our habits, aligned with the four elements:

1. Making the cue (**trigger**) obvious in good habits or invisible in bad.

2. Making the craving (**the need**) attractive in a good habit and unattractive in bad.

3. Making the response (**behaviour**) easy for a good habit and hard for a bad one.

4. Making the reward (**release** of emotional tension) satisfying in a good habit and unsatisfying in a bad one.

In the context of emotional overwhelm, the habit loop could look like this.b

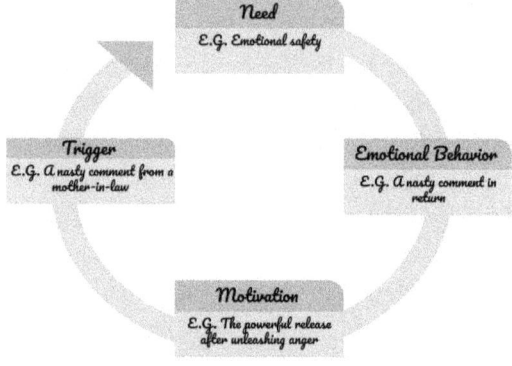

Figure 11 - Habit Loop in Emotional Overwhelm - Bad Habit

How to Make R.I.D.E. a Habit

Of course, good habits are possible too. It is not always easy, but all the elements of the Habit Loop can be made to work more in your favour.

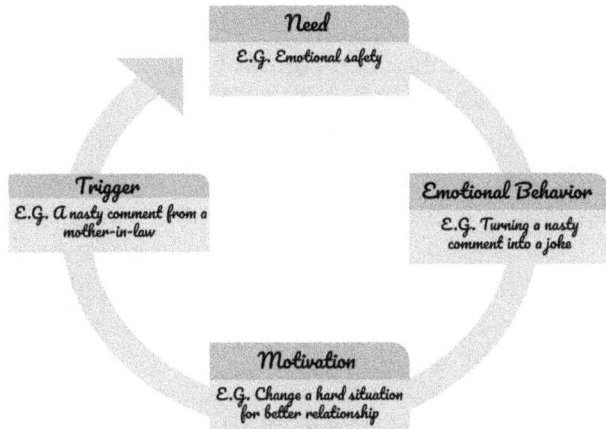

Figure 12 - Habit Loop in Emotional Overwhelm - Good Habit

For the purposes of internal habits, inversion laws — the negative side of the law — are risky. Many of us who have trouble with emotional overreactions already don't like that about ourselves - making those behaviours feel even worse can make us hate ourselves.

Except for **cue** (trigger), it is much better to work on the positive side of laws. As such, there are three ways to do this:

1. Work with the **cue** (trigger). Eliminate or prepare for it.

2. Make it easy to insert the new **response** (emotional behaviour).

3. Find a **reward** (motivation) powerful enough to pull you out of your **craving** (need).

#1 Work with Your Cue (Trigger)

The remarkable thing about most of our conflicts and arguments is how similar they feel. Despite the diversity of situations, people involved, issues, and feelings, the consistency of our responses and behaviours is notable. As we pick up various lessons through life, by the time we realize we have issues, we follow the same patterns repeatedly for years. It might be dating the same type of people, getting into the same arguments, falling apart at the same breakpoints — the list goes on.

Two key strategies that work with cues (triggers) are eliminating when possible and preparation when not.

Eliminate

Not all triggers in life can be easily eliminated, but many more than we think.

EXERCISE

> Detoxify your triggers:
>
> 1. Name at least three events that got you into a highly emotional state, potentially stressing you or at least making you feel terrible.
>
> 2. What are the similarities? Is it the same topic (For example, are you arguing about money with your client, your boss, and your partner) or with the

same person (For example, your brother-in-law makes you feel inadequate)?

3. Is there anything you can do to eliminate such situations or people from your life?

The examples could be:

1. Avoiding certain people or even eliminating them from your life. For example, if they only show up when they need something from you.

2. Avoid topics that trigger you. There is nothing wrong with talking about less intense things. For example, some people love to gossip, but such talk will drag you down and make you feel guilty, so why bother?

3. Think about your environment. Is there anything else that makes you stressed or edgy? If driving during rush hour makes you irritable and tired, why not leave earlier or agree with your boss to come in later? Or if you feel pressured that you need to pick up kids from school every day, can you have an alternative arrangement with your partner to bring them in the morning instead and then not rush in the evenings?

Be aware. Eliminating shouldn't be your strategy to avoid all problems in your life as this can backfire quickly. Eliminating is about not being vulnerable if you don't need to be, not about real-life problems that are better dealt with proactively.

> **PRO TIP.** Sameness and repetition are two key things that indicate where most habits lie, good or bad. Like Stephen R. Covey noted, 'Sow a thought, reap an action; sow an action, reap a habit; sow a habit, reap a character; sow a character, reap a destiny.'
>
> **Mistake to avoid**. Not pushing back enough. Most of us can change our environment much more than we think. We assume that we need to arrive at 9 if the job is 9 to 5, even if it means spending twice as much time on the road. We go to visit our relatives regularly even when they are mean to us. No rules are set in stone, so it's worth pushing hard enough against ones that land you in emotionally charged situations, like conflicts.

Prepare

The next best thing to elimination is preparation.

When you start observing patterns, you realize patterns follow bodily states. For example, I am one of the 'hangry' people. I know better than to schedule meetings just before lunch. I know I will snap or be cranky. After a bad night's sleep, my anxiety is through the roof, so a good sleep is a must before significant events. Even food matters. For example, sugary snacks increase sleepiness, so to be at your sharpest, eat a breakfast with eggs instead of a croissant. Finally, exercise and movement can work wonders to reduce your anxiety before a stressful event.

EXERCISE

1. **Prepare your body.** The more you know your body, the easier it becomes, but Sleep-Food-Exercise is a good place to start.

2. **Prepare your mind.** Meditation, breathing, or any mindfulness exercise helps you master your mind. Like reframing a stressful event as a learning opportunity, some fancier cognitive tools often require skill and practice. Start with breathing exercises. The '2-to-1 breath' technique I introduced in **Step 2** can be used as a preparation technique.

3. **Prepare your emotions.** One of the best ways to offset negative emotions is to have more positive ones. Of course, that's easier said than done, but knowing about upcoming stresses can help you purposefully invite more positive emotions.

For example, before a difficult meeting, I ensure I am well rested, hydrated, and full. I also seek out positive emotions on purpose. I go for a walk to soak up nature, have a cup of tea, or look at photos from a good weekend to remind me of happy moments. In other words, I will bring as many good emotions as possible as soon as possible to fill my emotional bank, knowing that my mind will be tested, or patience challenged.

Be aware. A cup of something hot to drink, a walk, and a quick chat will get you through the meeting but will not get you through a weekend with unfriendly in-laws. Keep that in mind when you're planning an event. A hot beverage wouldn't have been enough to manage the World Cup Finals pressure that Zidane experienced.

PRO TIP. Use a rule of thumb for 3:1 ratio of positive emotions to negative ones. The negative to positive ratio was first introduced by Barbara Fredrickson in her book *Positivity: Ground-breaking Research to Release Your Inner Optimist and Thrive*. Despite being discredited by other researchers, we know by human experience that our brains are often negatively biased, so we need to seek positivity to counter negativity purposefully and with more effort. The 3:1 ratio may not be scientifically probable but it's not a bad formula for attempting to attempt counter the negativity.

Mistake to avoid: Overthinking your emotions, whether positive or negative ones. Healthy emotions are generally short and don't stick around for long. Trying to keep the positive emotions longer can bring as much suffering as mulling over negative ones.

#2 Make it Easy to Insert a New Response (Behaviour)

There is a lot to say about the value of making new, healthier habits easy. Simplicity is at the core of R.I.D.E., with every step simplified, and easy to insert and apply. The better you know your **Emotional Footprint**, the easier it will be for you to insert new, healthier behaviours.

How to Make R.I.D.E. a Habit

The second part of making it easy is inserting the new response (more compassionate behaviour) to achieve the result in the quickest way possible. You do this in two steps. First, start small to make sure you see progress immediately. Just like you don't start surfing on 12-meter waves, you don't start mastering your emotions with the most intense situations, or biggest overwhelms. Second, celebrate progress to embed the new behaviour in your brain.

EXERCISE

> Three steps to making it easy to apply R.I.D.E.:
>
> 1. **Start small.** When you choose a situation to work on, choose something manageable. Every journey starts with the first step, and every house starts with the first brick. When you start small, you build on each step, each brick.
>
> 2. **Notice progress.** Change requires time, and when we fixate on short-term results, we can feel demotivated due to the perceived lack of progress. We often remember the most significant shifts in our lives, but one-off changes rarely cause them. They are usually an accumulation of many minor modifications along the way. Maybe you catch yourself not snapping at your child when they interrupted your focus—or perhaps not being too hard on yourself after an embarrassing situation. Ensure you record this progress — ideally, in a journal, but at a minimum, in your head. Noticing will keep you going, and it gets easier with every step.

3. **Celebrate your progress.** It's important to celebrate even if the simple wins to embed a new habit. A kind word to yourself after not snapping at an irritating colleague, noticing your frustration but not engaging in it. Savour the sense of achievement and contentment that comes with it. Next time you hold a meeting with various people wanting completely different things, reward yourself to celebrate your change. Rewarding yourself is one of the best ways to ensure you keep going!

Be aware. Inner achievements look different from external world actions and successes. Sometimes just noticing you feel different during incidents of emotional hijacking can be a success.

PRO TIP. Make a list of ten ways you will reward yourself. Make sure you have two types of rewards - one internal (e.g., kind words to yourself, feeling gratitude, or hugging yourself) and another external (a nice bath, watching pictures from you last trip or a massage). Use this list to reward yourself when you successfully manage an overwhelming situation.

Mistake to avoid. Demanding yourself to be in control all the time. Emotions make us human. No healthy person can keep their emotions in check all the time, so you shouldn't try for 100% either.

#3 Find a Better Reward (Motivation)

The simple fact is that you won't be able to master your emotions and behave in a more appropriate way *unless you want to*. Much of what drives emotional behaviour derives from a powerful need, such as to restore boundaries (anger), show you need help (with tears), or show remorse about violating social norms (turning red in the face from embarrassment). The need behind your emotional reaction needs to be attended for the healthier, less destructive, and more appropriate responses to work. To counter this strong pull, we need equally powerful pull (i.e., goals based on values) to invite better emotional responses.

EXERCISE

1. **Ask yourself why**. Why do you want to master emotional overwhelm?
   a. Do you want to stop losing your temper at work so that you are seen as a potential leader next time there is an opportunity for promotions?
   b. Do you want to stop crying when somebody criticizes you so that you are seen as strong and confident and get more responsibility?
   c. Do you want to stop panic attacks so that you are able to control your fear before important meetings?
   d. Do you want to stop showing your embarrassment so strongly so that you can have less awkward conversations?

e. Or do you want to get a hold of your emotional displays because you are sick and tired of people using your emotions against you?

There is no wrong answer here. Whatever works for you is the right answer (unless your answer is to manipulate someone else into doing something for you).

1. **Look for both intrinsic and extrinsic motivations.** Intrinsic ones are the most powerful. For example, I got so deep into emotional resilience because I didn't want to feel guilty and ashamed after losing my temper. While I wasn't too motivated by my emotional displays undermining my career, you might be motivated by a potential promotion or something else. The beauty of extrinsic motivations is that they are more visible and require more action, so it's good to have mixed goals.

2. **Make your goals clear and explicit.** Only clarity can help you remember what matters to you. Having clearly stated objectives will help you pull yourself in the right direction when you are in a stressful and emotional place.

Be aware. You might be tempted to choose goals based on what you 'should' or 'shouldn't' do or be. Remember, actions speak louder than words, so if you choose goals based on what you want to be rather than you already are, they might feel inauthentic, and they are unlikely to work.

> **PRO TIP**. The strongest hold is often related to our values. For example, you want to stop snapping at your kids because your family is at the top of your values hierarchy. It will work for you much better if you know it matters to you rather than trying not to lose your temper because it looks bad.
>
> **Mistake to avoid**. Going with 'logical' reasons over 'emotional' is unlikely to hold in emotionally charged situations. You might think that you are better off choosing your motivation for the most reasonable goal or value. The thing is, if your heart's not in it, it's unlikely to hold in the emotional overwhelm.
>
> Get your motivation clearly in front of you and remind yourself why you are doing this at all.

In this chapter, you learned a few ways to make R.I.D.E. a habit, but not everything can be changed. It is important to focus your energy where you can change. In the next chapter, you will learn where not to focus your energy.

Summary

1. Making R.I.D.E. a habit is your best chance of easy, near-automated emotional responses that are measured and serve you long-term.

2. The Habit Loop of cue (trigger), response (emotional behaviour), reward (better motivation), and craving (the need) can help you embed R.I.D.E. as a near-automatic response, making it easy to manage your emotions.

3. Avoiding or preparing for your triggers, finding stronger motivation (goals, values), and meeting emotional needs can help shape new and better emotional responses as a habit.

WHAT WE CAN AND CANNOT CHANGE

"Pick battles big enough to matter, small enough to win."
—Jonathan Kozol

The only time I lined up for anything newly released – including tickets, books, or iPhones - was for the last Harry Potter book. There is no surprise there - I am just one of the 500 million people who bought the books or another (probably) billion who watched the movies, borrowed the books, or read them in libraries.

The popularity of the series puzzled many, but anyone who reads them knows that J.K. Rowling is a true master of taking her readers for a ride with the heroes' emotions. Yes, the magic, the convenient at-the-end-of-school-year triumph of good over evil, and fun elements like quidditch helped too. But what captured so many of us was the emotional ride that Harry's journey offers. As long as we could feel his loneliness when living under the stairs, excitement about the new world he enters, or handle his concerns about high expectations for being special, we were hooked.

For a hero who saved the world seven school years in a row, Harry is remarkably prone to emotional hijacking. Within the first few weeks in a new school and magician world, he enters a fight with Malfoy, landing him in a duel. He also starts flying on his broom without first trying it even once - a hot-headed response that could have ended in a hospital stay. This behavioural pattern continues until his anger outbursts land him in the continuous punishment with Umbridge in book 5 and being banned from the quidditch team forever.

Compare Harry's hot-headedness to Hermione who, despite participating in most of the same events, keeps her cool to come back to Malfoy and others with intelligent comebacks and candid pranks. Hermione ensures they focus on long-term goals. One could argue it's because of her intelligence, but it's more likely that she simply has a different temperament.

Temperament cannot be underestimated when trying to manage ourselves in emotionally overwhelming situations because it has major influence on our reactions. For example, my best friend is one of the most even-tempered people I know, despite living in a high-paced US culture and working in a high-pressure corporate environment. I, however, can snap even when I am calm and rested, despite living in the 'no-worries' culture of Australia and having a less stressful job.

Environmental and social influences, how your family displays emotions, past experiences and memories, and even personal communication preferences can impact how we respond when overwhelmed. Trying to untangle this multitude of factors is impossible, and even if we managed to separate them, it might take decades to bring changes. Since we need solutions to our emotionally driven behaviours now, it's better to focus on what we can change and not worry about what we can't.

Genetics

Sonya Lyubomirsky, a well-renowned happiness researcher, suggests that our happiness levels depend approximately 50% on genes and 50% on other factors, like the environment[34]. Notably, Dr. Lyubomirsky warns about taking these percentages too seriously, but it's a good rule of thumb to know. Just like we can't choose our parents, the colour of our eyes, or long legs, we cannot choose our temperaments. I never was able to change my sensitivity, no matter how hard I tried. The only thing I changed is my ability to manage it and even embrace it. It's better to make the most of what we have than to spend our energy fighting who we are.

Cultural and Social Influences

The way we grow up shapes us in conscious and unconscious ways. Our parents and extended families talked, acted, and resolved their conflicts in front of us, embedding their values, worldviews, and behaviours in ways barely noticeable to us. What we saw growing up had an enormous impact on how we behave, react, and resolve disputes now.

The cultural and societal background put another layer of influence on our behaviours. Despite growing up in a loving family, I was shaped by the tough Eastern European culture. Zidane is probably shaped by his French-Arabic ancestry and family values, and Marco by his experiences growing up in Italy, which influenced how that situation with the headbutt unfolded. In his book, Marco notes, 'I don't understand why it got such a reaction from him: I've heard much worse growing up.'

As a sensitive person who barely uttered a word before school, borrowing her sister's social connections until then, I probably would have grown up to be someone very different in a more safe, easy-going, and nurturing culture. But just like I can't undo the harshness of my cultural influence, Zidane and Marco can't change theirs – we all can only try to make the most of it.

Life Circumstances

In some cases, our environment is controlled by other people so much that we don't have a lot of choice in our decisions, and that impacts our behaviour. Prison is an extreme example of this, but even in normal life, we have restrictions. For example, many children are mainly under the control of their parents about what they eat, what they can and cannot do, where they live, even who they hang out with. Parents have restrictions related to money, family responsibilities, and a hundred other things. Instead of focusing on those restrictions, we can focus on doing our best within them. We don't always realize our power, but we often can do more than we think — remove or limit exposure to toxic people, practice saying no to things that exhaust us, and change jobs when we are bullied.

Rather than fighting everything we are and everything that shaped us, we can pick our battles.

Summary

1. There are limits to what we can change — at least in a short time. You are better off knowing what you can and what you can't influence and focusing your efforts on where they can bring the most change.

2. Genetics, social and cultural influences, and life circumstances are just a few things that might be outside of your control.

3. Accepting those factors that are hard or even impossible to change is the first step to deciding what you can and want to change in the future.

FINAL NOTE

I do not forget that my voice is but one voice, my experience in a mere drop in the sea, my knowledge no greater than the visual field in a microscope, my mind's eye a mirror that reflects a small concern of the world and my ideas - a subjective confession.

- C.C. Jung, Modern Man in Search of a Soul.

If one of the greatest minds of the 20th century considered his ideas just a subjective drop in the sea back in 1933, how much can a book of a working professional in 2021 matter, where published word competes with machines? Less than a grain of sand, most likely.

And yet, I felt compelled to write this book.

I know that not everyone experiences the world as I do. The world of an HSP — a highly sensitive person — can become 'too much' at almost any second. Light, sounds, people, or a cup of strong coffee can overwhelm me quickly and intensely. But I doubt that Zidane is an HSP. Or Dan

Harris and Andrew Marr, for that matter. In his biographical book *10 Percent Happier*, Dan Harris admits that his struggles after reporting in Afghanistan related not to trauma but to the lack of adrenaline in his everyday life. Does that sound like a sensitive person to you?

How come, despite being such different people with different cultural experiences, we have such similar overwhelming behaviours? How come we see so many people struggling to control their emotions on T.V., during sports, at work, and in parliaments? How come we feel paralyzed, hyperventilate, unleash our anger or let our embarrassment decide how we live? How come we resort to 'just breathe,' 'suck it up,' and 'search for root cause' so often?

We probably look for help in the wrong places. Yes, our mind is powerful, but it is only a part of who we are. Just like I can't wish away my rheumatoid arthritis by simply thinking positively, I can't control my emotions by simply deciding. I can suppress, numb, or avoid them, but none of those strategies hold up for long, and the price to pay is high — exhaustion, feeling numb and empty, or breakdowns.

What I've come to understand is that solutions that rely on one thing only — thoughts, emotions, or body — will always leave me weaker, not stronger. When you rely on only part of you to carry you forward, you never feel whole.

And this is the thought I want to leave you with. Try R.I.D.E. or not. Accept your emotions or not. Go with whatever tools work for you. But whatever you do, go for solutions that accept your whole fabulous self — emotions, body, and thoughts — not the ones that poke holes in it.

That is the only way to be in control of yourself – your complete self.

SUMMARIES

How Do We Get Emotionally Overwhelmed?

1. Amygdala hijacking is a process that bypasses the slower, perspective-taking parts of the brain to respond quickly and ensure our survival.

2. Modern life has much fewer external threats but many more social ones. These social threats are more complex and take longer to resolve, giving us time to formulate better responses.

3. 'Emotional hijacking' explains why it is so hard to stop ourselves in the midst of a heated moment, but 'emotional overwhelm' better captures the slower, tamer reaction that better suits social threats.

R.I.D.E. - Four Steps Out of Emotional Overwhelm

1. To successfully change your behaviour in an emotionally charged situation, you need to know your body's signs and learn to read them to prevent behavioural disasters.

2. R.I.D.E. lies on the assumption that your body, thoughts, and emotions are valuable sources of information that you can apply to master self-control in a healthier and genuinely lasting way, rather than suppression of, avoidance of, or distraction from your emotions.

3. The power of R.I.D.E. rides in using positive emotions to counter negative ones, instead of fighting them. Positive emotions broaden our view, reduce emotional intensity, and encourage prosocial be-

haviours, all of which helps us to pull out of the situation that is dominated by negative, intense emotions, pre-conscious thoughts and urges, and anti-social behaviours.

Be Aware of These Three Traps

1. Decades can be lost on unwinnable arguments, proving subjective truths, or pointing fingers.
2. The question that matters is. 'Are your emotional responses helpful or hurtful?'
3. Life has its ways to settle scores. You don't need to do its job.

Step 1: R. - Recognize the signs early

1. To get out of emotional overwhelm, you need to recognize your body and mind's signs. The triangle tool helps capture those signs specific to you so that you can recognize them early and change the course of your behaviour.
2. The six case studies of emotional overwhelm are closely related to six basic emotions that are near-universal in humans.
3. The signs of emotional overwhelm are briefness, intensity, and destructive impact, internal or external.

Step 2: I. - Imitate A Relaxed Body State

1. I. is about imitating a relaxed state to reduce emotional overwhelm in your body and give you time to insert appropriate responses.

2. Using your body and posture at the same time maximizes your chances of reducing your physiological response to emotional overwhelm, giving you more time.

3. Alternative strategies, like visualization or muscle relaxation, can be powerful but require more practice and preparation to work.

Step 3: D – Deploy Self-Compassion

1. D. is about deploying self-compassion as a positive force to counter an overwhelmingly negative one, and doing it with mindfulness, kindness, and searching for common humanity.

2. Feeling more during the emotional overwhelm sounds counterintuitive, but it works quicker than suppression, reasoning, or other cognitive approaches that exhaust us.

3. By using a 'third-person' technique, we can increase distance from the situation without overloading ourselves mentally.

Step 4: E – Evoke Connection

1. E. is about **evoking connection** with people in an intense situation to bring in a strong positive emotion, compassion, to replace a strong negative one.

2. Self-control usually includes other people, therefore social emotions do a great job of switching the perspective from 'me' to 'we.'

3. Compassion also helps us manage the need for immediate gratification, like venting, that makes self-control possible and even easy.

R.I.D.E. In Practise

1. R.I.D.E. is a tool that can get you out of emotional hijacking or highly emotional situations in seconds.

2. The tool can be applied in various situations, with most intense emotions, without putting too much strain on your cognitive load.

3. The power of R.I.D.E. is not just in simplicity, but in the practise.

What Successful Emotional Control Looks Like

1. While neither R.I.D.E. nor any other tool guarantees 100% success, celebrating the signs of success, no matter how small, will keep you going.

2. The ultimate mastery of emotional overwhelm is not successful suppression or feeling less; it's the ability to handle your emotions but show them appropriately.

3. Even the most minor signs of success, like recognizing the signs in your body, will help you unlock the other levels.

How to Make R.I.D.E. a Habit

1. Making R.I.D.E. a habit is your best chance of easy, near-automated emotional responses that are measured and serve you long-term.

2. The Habit Loop of cue (trigger), response (emotional behaviour), reward (better motivation), and craving (the need) can help you embed R.I.D.E. as a near-automatic response, making it easy to manage your emotions.

3. Avoiding or preparing for your triggers, finding stronger motivation (goals, values), and meeting emotional needs can help shape new and better emotional responses as a habit.

What We Can and Cannot Change

1. There are limits to what we can change — at least in a short time. You are better off knowing what you can and what you can't influence and focusing your efforts on where they can bring the most change.

2. Genetics, social and cultural influences, and life circumstances are just a few things that might be outside of your control.

3. Accepting those factors that are hard or even impossible to change is the first step to deciding what you can and want to change in the future.

ABOUT ME

 I created Emotionready.com because I want to offer an alternative story about emotions - one where they are not a nuisance to dismiss, but useful tools to progress our goals in life.

A life spent suppressing & minimizing what we feel is a diminished one. It can be a dull, numb affair without the highs and lows that emotions bring. It can lead us to values we don't connect with, make us chase fake goals, and never get what we actually want.

I know an alternative. I've enjoyed it myself.

In that alternative, emotions are neither good nor bad, but pieces of information that can be put to use. As long as we manage them to prevent them from overwhelming us, getting stuck in them, or expressing them inappropriately, emotions can guide us towards our goals faster, more directly, and with more energy.

Emotional intelligence to me is not a new leadership fad, but a crucial life skill. At the core of this skill is recognizing, managing, and using our emotions intelligently.

If you want to hear more about how to do that and help you advance your goals, read more on emotionready.com contact me directly at lina@emotionready.com.

About me

If you want to hear more about how to switch emotions from being your enemy to your friend, visit emotionready.com, sign up for newsletters, or follow on:

facebook.com/emotionready

pinterest.com/emotionready

linaj.medium.com/

TABLE OF FIGURES

Figure 1 - 6 Typical Cognitive Distortions	41
Figure 2 - Emotion Wheel	42
Figure 3 - Emotional Footprint of Anger	44
Figure 4 - Emotional Footprint of Fear	47
Figure 5 - Emotional Footprint of Embarrassment	48
Figure 6 - Emotional Footprint of Sadness	50
Figure 7 - Emotional Footprint of Shock	51
Figure 8 - Emotional Footprint of Joy	52
Figure 9 - Emotional Footprint BLANK	53
Figure 10 - Emotional Footprint of Calm	60
Figure 11 - Habit Loop in Emotional Overwhelm - Bad Habit	98
Figure 12 - Habit Loop in Emotional Overwhelm - Good Habit	99

ENDNOTES

1. Bergland, C. (2017), Diaphragmatic Breathing Exercises and Your Vagus Nerve. Retrieved from https://www.psychologytoday.com/au/blog/the-athletes-way/201705/diaphragmatic-breathing-exercises-and-your-vagus-nerve

2. Van Sijk, S. (2013). *DBT Made Simple*. Oakland, CA: New Harbinger Publications.

3. Desteno, D. (2019). Emotional Success : The Power of Gratitude, Compassion, and Pride. *Compassion Builds Inner Strength and Inner Peace* (pp. 81-114). Boston, United States: Houghton Mifflin Harcourt Publishing Company.

4. Schroeder, O.M. (2017). The Physical and Mental Toll of Being Angry All the Time. Retrieved from https://health.usnews.com/wellness/mind/articles/2017-10-26/the-physical-and-mental-toll-of-being-angry-all-the-time

5. Six Seconds: The Emotional Intelligence Network. (2020). Retrieved from: https://www.6seconds.org/

6. Berkeley University of California University (Producer). (2020). *Empathy and Emotional Intelligence at Work* [EdX]. Retrieved from https://www.edx.org/course/empathy-and-emotional-intelligence-at-work

7. Taylor, J.B. (2009). *My stroke of Insight*. Penguin Books.

8. AAA Foundation for Traffic Safety. (2016). *Prevalence of Self-Reported Aggressive Driving Behavior: United States, 2014 (*Technical Report). Washington, D.C.: AAA Foundation for Traffic Safety.

9. Haghighatdoost, F., Feizi, A., Esmaillzadeh, A., Rashidi-Pourfard, N., Keshteli, A.H., Roohafza, F., and Payman Adibi (2018). Drinking plain water is associated with decreased risk of depression and anxiety in adults: Results from a large cross-sectional study. *World Journal of Psychiatry, 8(3): 88–96.* doi: 10.5498/wjp.v8.i3.88

10. Chen, A. (2018). How Hunger Pangs Can Make Nice People 'Hangry'. Retrieved from https://www.npr.org/sections/health-shots/2018/06/11/618395072/how-hunger-pangs-can-make-nice-people-hangry

11. Fredrickson, B.L. (1998). What good are positive emotions? *Review of General Psychology. ;2:*300–319. Retrieved from https://journals.sage-

pub.com/doi/full/10.1037/1089-2680.2.3.300?casa_token=yZ-LWnvy1kYAAAAA%3AH71feAYP2-YH7NM9-Jg2S7WzytRjm9gWmH914GlSSdultfSjS6beazVuolVisPSJtwZuj7drsfK1zg

12. Aknin, L. & Van de Vondervoort, J., and Hamlin, J.K.. (2017). Positive Feelings Reward and Promote Prosocial Behavior. *Current Opinion in Psychology. 20.* 10.1016/j.copsyc.2017.08.017.

13. Méndez-Bértolo, C., Moratti, S., Toledano, R., Lopez-Sosa, F., Martínez-Alvarez, R., Mah, Y.H., Vuilleumier, P., Gil-Nagel, A., and Strange, B.A. (2016). A fast pathway for fear in human amygdala. *Nature Neuroscience,* doi: 10.1038/nn.4324

14. Hietanen, J., Glerean, E. & Hari, R. and Nummenmaa, L. (2016). Bodily maps of emotions across child development. *Developmental Science. 19.* n/a-n/a. 10.1111/desc.12389

    Figure 2. Bodily topography of basic emotions associated with the six basic emotions and neutral state. Reprinted from "Bodily maps of emotions across child development," by Hietanen, J., Glerean, E. & Hari, R. and Nummenmaa, L., 2016, *Developmental Science. 19.* Retrieved from https://www.researchgate.net/publication/295542402_Bodily_maps_of_emotions_across_child_development.

15. Segerstrom, S. (2011). The structure and consequences of repetitive thought. *Psychological Science Agenda.* Retrieved from bhttps://www.apa.org/science/about/psa/2011/03/repetitive-thought

16. Greenberg, L. (2015). Emotion-Focused Therapy : Coaching Clients to Work Through Their Feelings. *Evaluating whether a painful primary emotion is healthy* (pp. 172-192). Washington DC, United States: American Psychological Association

17. Smih, J.A. (2015).What is the Relationship Between Stress and Empathy? Retrieved from https://greatergood.berkeley.edu/article/item/what_is_the_relationship_between_stress_and_empathy

18. Rosenberg, J. (2019). *90 Seconds to a Life You Love : How to Turn Difficult Feelings into Rock-Solid Confidence.* London, United Kingdom: Hodder & Stoughton.

19. Bergland, C. (2017). Diaphragmatic Breathing Exercises and Your Vagus Nerve. Retrieved from https://www.psychologytoday.com/au/blog/the-athletes-way/201705/diaphragmatic-breathing-exercises-and-your-vagus-nerve

Endnotes

20 Park, A. (2017). This Is the Fastest Way to Calm Down. Retrieved from https://time.com/4718723/deep-breathing-meditation-calm-anxiety/

21 Elsesser, K. (2018).Power Posing Is Back: Amy Cuddy Successfully Refutes Criticism. Retrieved from https://www.forbes.com/sites/kimelsesser/2018/04/03/power-posing-is-back-amy-cuddy-successfully-refutes-criticism/?sh=a0a38f63b8ef

22 Marmolejo-Ramos, F., Murata, A., Sasaki, K., Yamada, Y., Ikeda, A., Hinojosa, J. A., Watanabe, K., Parzuchowski, M., Tirado, C., & Ospina, R. (2020). Your face and moves seem happier when I smile: Facial action influences the perception of emotional faces and biological motion stimuli. Experimental Psychology, 67(1), 14–22. https://doi.org/10.1027/1618-3169/a000470

23 Erik Peper, I-Mei Lin; Increase or Decrease Depression: How Body Postures Influence Your Energy Level. *Biofeedback* 1 September 2012; 40 (3): 125–130. doi:.org/10.5298/1081-5937-40.3.01

24 Wilkes, C., Kydd, R., Sagar, M., Broadbent, E. (2017). Upright posture improves affect and fatigue in people with depressive symptoms. *Journal of Behavior Therapy and Experimental Psychiatry*, Volume 54, doi.org/10.1016/j.jbtep.2016.07.015.

25 Gilkey, R, and Kilts, C. (2017). Cognitive Fitness. In: On Mental Toughness, Harvard Business Review, p. 48-52.

26 Zargarzadeh, M., & Shirazi, M. (2014). The effect of progressive muscle relaxation method on test anxiety in nursing students. I*ranian journal of nursing and midwifery research, 19(6), 607–612.*

27 Sharifah Maimunah, S.M., Hashim, H.A. (2016). Differential Effects of 7 and 16 Groups of Muscle Relaxation Training Following Repeated Submaximal Intensity Exercise in Young Football Players. Percept Mot Skills. 122(1):227-37. doi: 10.1177/*0031512515625383*

28 Greenberg, L. (2015). Emotion-Focused Therapy : Coaching Clients to Work Through Their Feelings. *Epilogue* (pp. 349-353). Washington DC, United States: American Psychological Association

29 Gross, J.J. (2015). Handbook of Emotion Regulation. *Emotion Regulation: Conceptual and Empirical Foundations* (pp.3-23). Guilford Publications.

30 Khazan, O. (2018). Better Than Willpower. Retrieved from https://www.theatlantic.com/science/archive/2018/01/willpower-isnt-the-best-way-to-get-things-done/550766/

31 Harris, D. (2014). 10% Happier: How I Tamed the Voice in My Head, Reduced Stress Without Losing My Edge, and Found Self-Help That Actually Works--A True Story. Dey Street Books.

32 Harmon, S. (2020, February 7). Julia Gillard's misogyny speech voted 'most unforgettable' moment in Australian TV history. *The Guardian*. Retrieved from https://www.theguardian.com/tv-and-radio/2020/feb/07/julia-gillard-misogyny-speech-voted-most-unforgettable-moment-in-australian-tv-history

33 Science Daily (2013). Healthy habits die hard: In times of stress, people lean on established routines -- even healthy ones.

Retrieved from https://www.sciencedaily.com/releases/2013/05/130527100620.htm

34 Lyubomirsky, S., Sheldon, K.M., and Schkade, D. (2005). Pursuing Happiness: The Architecture of Sustainable Change. *Review of General Psychology*. Vol. 9, No. 2, 111–131. doi: 10.1037/1089-2680.9.2.11

www.ingramcontent.com/pod-product-compliance
Lightning Source LLC
Chambersburg PA
CBHW061329040426
42444CB00011B/2825